Countries Around the World

France

Mary Colson

Raintree is an imprint of **Capstone Global Library Limited**, a company incorporated in England and Wales having its registered office at 7 Pilgrim Street, London, EC4V 6LB – Registered company number: 6695582

First published in hardback in 2012

Edited by Louise Galpine, Kate DeVilliers, and Laura Knowles
Designed by Richard Parker
Original illustrations © Capstone Global Library Ltd 2011
Illustrated by Oxford Designers & Illustrators
Picture research by Liz Alexander
Originated by Capstone Global Library Ltd
Printed in China by CTPS

ISBN 978 1 406 22800 7 (hardback)
15 14 13 12 11
10 9 8 7 6 5 4 3 2 1

British Library Cataloguing in Publication Data
Colson, Mary.
France. -- (Countries around the world)
1. France--Juvenile literature.
944'.084-dc22
A full catalogue record for this book is available from the British Library.

Acknowledgments
We would like to thank the following for permission to reproduce photographs: Alamy p. **12** (© Photos 12); Corbis pp. **10** (© The Gallery Collection), **24** (© POOL/Reuters), **33** (© Tim De Waele/TDWsport.com), **35** (© Riviere/photocuisine); Getty Images pp. **21** (David C Tomlinson/Photographer's Choice), **29** (Sylvain Sonnet/Photographer's Choice); iStockphoto pp. **9** (© Chris Dawson), **15** (© Christoph Achenbach), **27** (© Paul Fawcett); Photolibrary pp. **6** (R H Productions), **7** (peter schickert), **18** (Alain Le Bot/Photononstop), **20** (Henry Ausloos), **23** (Stéphane Ouzounoff), **30** (Ernst Wrba); Shutterstock pp. **5** (© Jean-Edouard Rozey), **8** (© Worakit Sirijinda), **17** (© PHB.cz (Richard Semik)), **26** (© Baloncici), **31** (© Mikhail Zahranichny), **37** (© Paul Reid), **46** (© Route66), **34** (© PixAchi).

Cover photograph of tourists with red umbrellas near the Eiffel Tower reproduced with permission of Corbis/© Owen Franken.

We would like to thank Rob Bowden for his invaluable help in the preparation of this book.

Disclaimer
All the Internet addresses (URLs) given in this book were valid at the time of going to press. However, due to the dynamic nature of the Internet, some addresses may have changed, or sites may have changed or ceased to exist since publication. While the author and publisher regret any inconvenience this may cause readers, no responsibility for any such changes can be accepted by either the author or the publisher.

Contents

Some words are printed in bold, **like this**. You can find out what they mean by looking in the glossary.

Introducing France

What comes into your mind when you think of France? Do you see the Eiffel Tower and art galleries? Or do you think of delicious cakes, cheese, and designer clothes?

France is the largest country in Western Europe and is famous as an artistic, stylish, and cultural nation with fantastic art, great literature, and fine wines. The landscape is equally impressive with dramatic mountains, deep river gorges, rugged coastlines, and beautiful beaches.

Politics and power

France is one of the places where the European Parliament meets, and is at the heart of European politics. It is a member of the **G8** group of wealthiest countries. France once had an **empire**, which included land in America, Africa, and in the Pacific. The national flag is called the Tricolore and is three vertical stripes of blue, white, and red.

Language guardians

The *Académie Française* protects French **culture** and language. There are strict laws to ensure that most TV programmes are French language in origin and not subtitled or **dubbed** from other languages.

How to say...

French people greet each other by kissing on both cheeks. French people say "bonjour" as a general greeting to other people, for example when they go into a shop.

good day	*bonjour*	(bon-jure)
how are you?	*ça va?*	(sa va)
I'm fine, thanks	*ça va bien, merci*	(sa va bee-an, mur-see)
my name is…	*Je m'appelle…*	(juh map-el)
see you later	*a tout à l'heure*	(a toot a ler)
bye	*au revoir*	(oh re-vwa)

France is truly spectacular. Villages perched on hilltops look out over deep valleys and farmland.

History: Romans, revolution, republic

France is named after the Franks, a **tribe** of people who lived in central Europe. Their ruler, Clovis (around AD 466–511), went to war against the Romans and eventually reigned over what is now France. He also changed his religious beliefs and became a **Roman Catholic**.

Expanding empire

By the 10th century, the Franks governed most of Belgium, Holland, and parts of western Germany. In 1066, the French nobleman William of Normandy invaded England. He defeated the English king Harold II at the Battle of Hastings and was crowned King of England on Christmas Day.

From 1066 until 1558, France and England fought over French land and the throne. One of the most famous battles during this time was the Battle of Agincourt, won by England in 1415. In 1558, France regained Calais, the last French port held by the English. The two countries have remained separate ever since.

The Bayeux Tapestry tells the story of the Norman conquest of England in 1066.

The Romans built this Amphitheatre in the town of Orange. Plays and concerts are still performed there today.

Faith wars

In the 16th century, French Catholics and **Protestants** fought each other over their faith. In 1572, the Catholic queen ordered a day of killing known as the St Bartholomew's Day **Massacre**. Hundreds of Protestants were killed. In 1598, the **Edict** of Nantes granted religious freedom.

Daily life

Throughout the 17th and 18th centuries, poor families survived by working as farm labourers or as servants in the **chateaux** of the rich. Even children were sent out to work. In the evenings, women did sewing work to earn a few extra coins to help feed their family.

Cultural and political revolutions

The 18th century was a golden era in French art and science. It was a period of **extravagance** for the French **monarchy**. King Louis XIV had a luxurious palace built at Versailles.

Louis' grandson, Louis XVI, spent even more money. An unfair **tax** system meant that poorer workers paid the most whilst the richer **nobles** paid little or no tax. A dangerous feeling of unrest was growing among the poor.

The Palace of Versailles is just outside Paris.

Daily life

The winter of 1788–1789 was especially cold. Frozen rivers stopped people from transporting food. The cost of food rose dramatically and people were starving. By July, their anger had reached boiling point.

Long live the Republic!

The night of 14 July 1789 changed France forever. Thousands of angry peasants marched through the streets of Paris crying out "Freedom!" and "Equality!" They stormed the hated Bastille prison and freed the prisoners inside. It was the start of the French Revolution.

The Revolution was a battle for equal rights for everyone. The poor wanted a **republic**, a country with an **elected** government and no king or queen. The rich wanted to keep their privileged lifestyles and avoid taxes. Thousands of rich and poor died during the bloody revolution. Louis XVI and his queen Marie-Antoinette were executed by **guillotine** in 1793, along with many other nobles.

Bastille Day is on 14 July. It is a public holiday in France.

An emperor and an empire

After the Revolution, there was a **power vacuum** in France. In 1799, General Napoleon Bonaparte seized control. Napoleon was a military **genius**. He had spent much of his early army career abroad in Italy and Egypt helping to expand the French **Empire**. Once in power, he changed the tax system to make it fairer.

Empire building

In 1804, Napoleon crowned himself emperor and set about creating a vast empire. Between 1804 and 1811, French armies gained territory in Africa, America, and Europe. Emperor Napoleon seemed unstoppable.

This painting of Napoleon Bonaparte shows him leading his troops over the Alps into Italy.

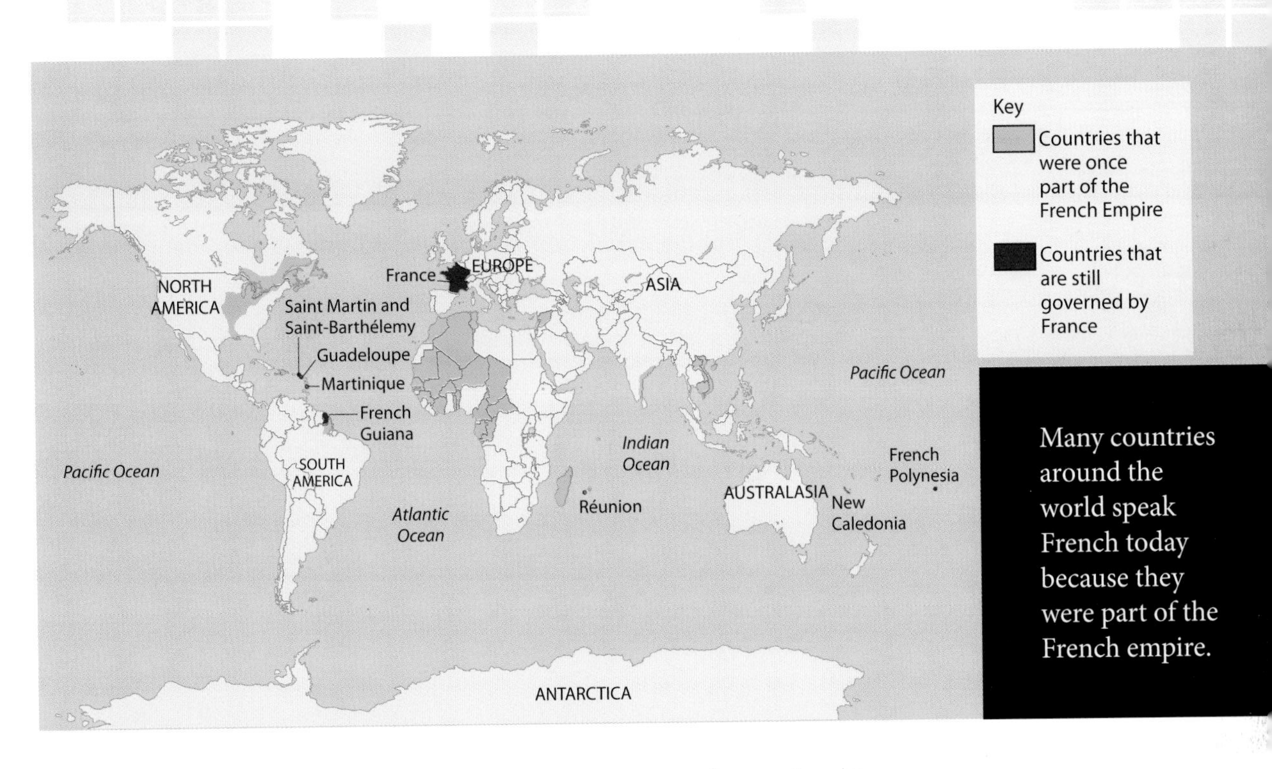

Many countries around the world speak French today because they were part of the French empire.

Other European countries, such as Britain, were determined to stop Napoleon's plans. A series of wars led to Napoleon's eventual defeat at the Battle of Waterloo in 1815. Napoleon was **exiled** to the Mediterranean island of St Helena and Louis XVIII, brother of the executed Louis XVI, took the throne.

France continued as a monarchy until 1848 when a series of bloody revolutions across Europe saw working people demand equal rights and political change. By the turn of the 20th century, despite political upheaval and social unrest, France had expanded into Southeast Asia and the Pacific islands. The empire was still growing.

VICTOR HUGO (1802–1885)

Victor Hugo was a poet, playwright, and novelist. He wrote the story of *The Hunchback of Notre Dame*. He also wrote *Les Misérables*, which is set in the time leading up to the 1848 revolution. The story has been turned into a world famous musical.

War and peace

In the last 100 years, French **culture** has influenced global fashion, film, and science. French people, though, have twice witnessed the horrors of war on their own soil.

During World War I (1914–1918) many battles were fought in **trenches**. At the Battle of the Somme, over 700,000 soldiers died. Britain, the United States, and other European countries helped defeat Germany in 1918.

Daily life

Life in the trenches was a daily fight for survival. Soldiers had to dodge **sniper** bullets, enemy bombs, and diseases carried by thousands of rats. Lice bred in their dirty clothes and caused unbearable itching. The cold and wet conditions also caused **trench foot**. If untreated, it could result in **amputation**.

During World War II, French Resistance fighters blew up railways to disrupt German supply lines.

LUCIE AUBRAC (1912–2007)

Lucie Aubrac was a member of the French Resistance. She helped to run the secret newspaper *Libération (Freedom)*. This told people what the Resistance was doing to fight the Germans.

In 1939, World War II began. In 1940, Adolf Hitler's German forces conquered Paris. The north and west parts of France were occupied until 1944. Secretly, General Charles de Gaulle organized the **Resistance** movement from London. When the war ended in 1945, de Gaulle briefly became leader of France, and was later president from 1959 to 1969.

A new direction

In the second half of the 20th century, many of France's **colonies**, such as Algeria and Vietnam, gained independence. Today, France no longer has an empire. Many people from its former colonies come to live in France, making it a very **multicultural** country.

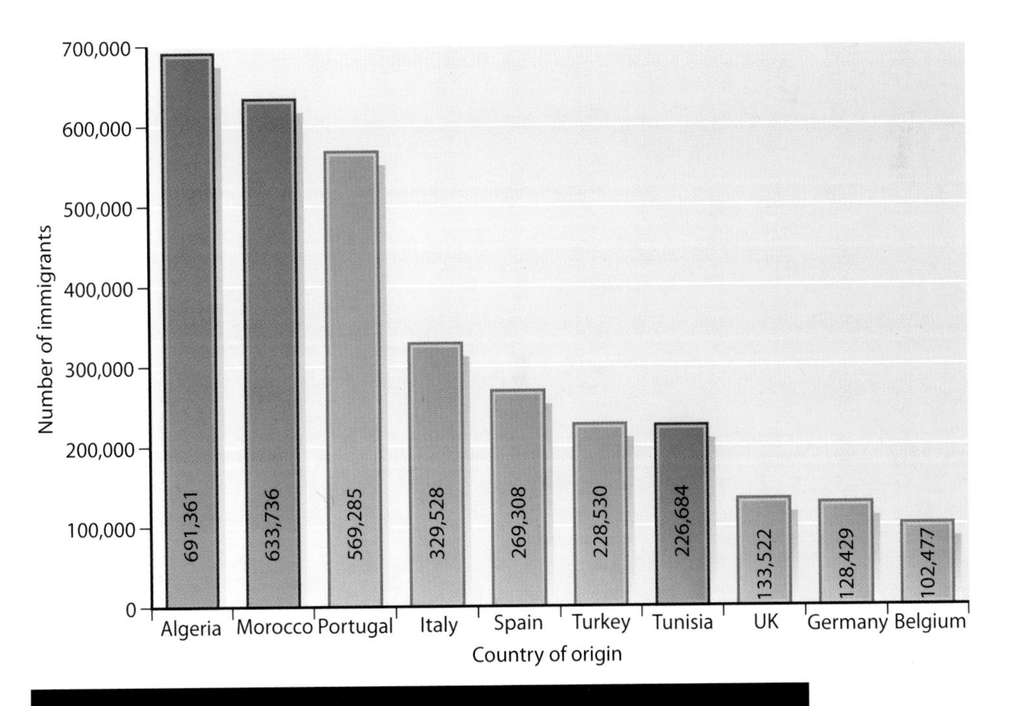

This bar chart shows the top 10 countries that immigrants living in France have come from, based on a survey in 2006. The red bars represent former French colonies.

Regions and resources: landscape and living

France is a diverse country with mountains, beaches, **dormant** volcanoes, and fertile farmland. Over a quarter of the country is forest. There are five mountain ranges including the Alps, the Pyrenees, and the Massif Central, a spectacular chain of extinct volcanoes. Mont Blanc in the Alps is Europe's highest mountain at 4,810 metres (15,780 feet).

This map shows the key landscape features of France.

Weather report

The French climate is mild with monthly averages between 3 and 19 °Celsius (37 and 66 °Fahrenheit). The north is cooler than the south, with the Alps the coldest place in winter. Along the Mediterranean coast, summer temperatures are high, making this area one of Europe's most popular holiday destinations.

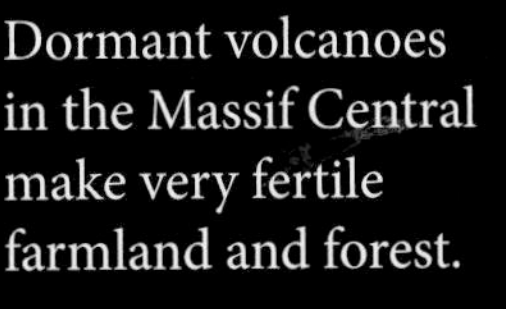

Dormant volcanoes in the Massif Central make very fertile farmland and forest.

Neighbours and numbers

Bordered by Spain, Germany, Italy, Belgium, Switzerland, Monaco, Andorra, and Luxembourg, France is home to 64 million people who live in about 550,000 square kilometres (210,000 square miles) of land. Because of its shape, France is also known as "the hexagon".

France governs four countries overseas. They are French Guiana, Martinique, Guadaloupe, and Réunion.

There are five main rivers in France. The longest river is the Loire at 1,020 kilometres (634 miles), followed by the Rhine, the Rhône, the Seine, and the Garonne. The four seas around the coast are the Mediterranean, the North Sea, the English Channel, and the Atlantic Ocean.

How to say...

river	*la fleuve*	(la flerve)
beach	*la plage*	(la plarge)
mountain	*la montagne*	(la montan)
sea	*la mer*	(la mair)
lake	*le lac*	(luh lak)
forest	*la forêt*	(la foray)
coast	*la côte*	(la cot)
valley	*la vallée*	(la valay)

Regional character

France is divided into 22 administrative regions, which are then divided into smaller departments. The richest region is the Ile-de-France, which includes Paris. Each region has its own character, traditions, cuisine, and flag. Some have their own **dialect**. In Brittany, some people speak Breton.

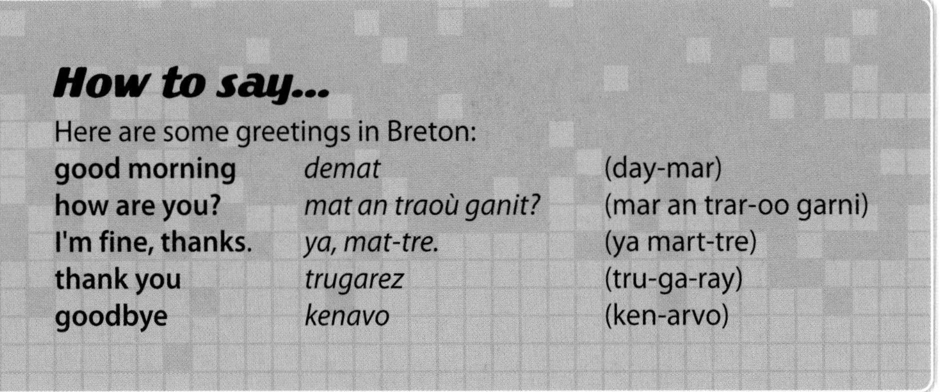

How to say...

Here are some greetings in Breton:

good morning	*demat*	(day-mar)
how are you?	*mat an traoù ganit?*	(mar an trar-oo garni)
I'm fine, thanks.	*ya, mat-tre.*	(ya mart-tre)
thank you	*trugarez*	(tru-ga-ray)
goodbye	*kenavo*	(ken-arvo)

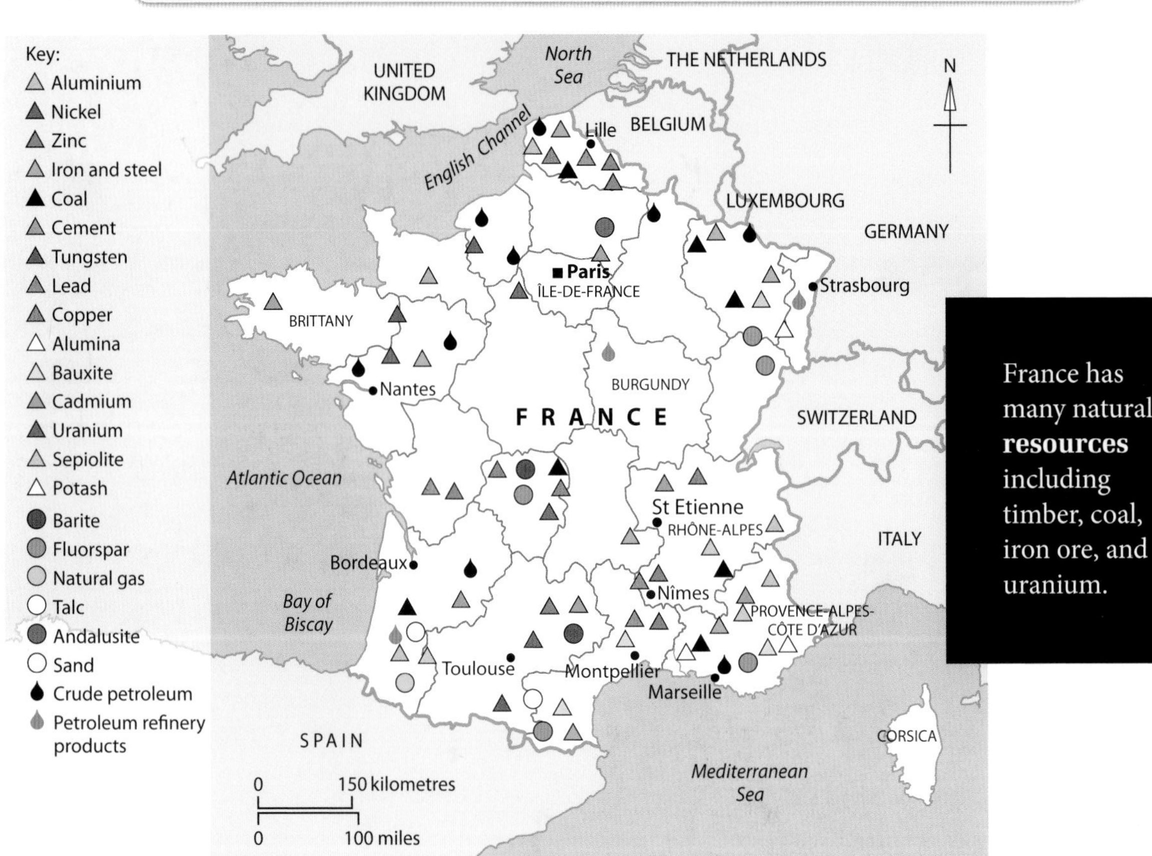

France has many natural **resources** including timber, coal, iron ore, and uranium.

These sunflower fields are in Provence, southern France.

A nation of farmers

Different regions specialize in different crops depending on climate and soil. Brittany is the main vegetable-growing region, while Rhône-Alps is a key dairy-farming area. The vineyards that make French wine are mostly in Burgundy and Bordeaux. Sunny Provence is the main flower, olive, and orchard area.

Factory towns

The industrial centres of France are mainly in the north and centre. Large chemical factories, textile mills, and food processing plants dominate the towns of Lille, Paris, and St Etienne. Nîmes, in the south, has a large cloth industry and is where denim comes from. The word *denim* means "de Nîmes" or "from Nîmes".

Daily life

In the cities, people mostly live in tall, modern blocks of flats. In the countryside, where there is more space, people often build their own houses. In the mountains, people live in traditional wooden chalets. Many houses have shutters outside the windows for extra security and to keep the rooms inside cool.

Economic status

France has one of the largest **economies** in the world, worth over £1.2 trillion per year. It is in the eurozone of 16 European countries that use the euro as **currency**. The symbol of the euro is €. The average income per person in France is around £20,500.

Industrial strength

France has a workforce of 28 million people. Large employers include the national airline, Air France, and car companies Renault and Peugeot. The world's largest airliner, the Airbus 380, is built in France. French factories produce 250,000 cars every month.

High-tech factories employ thousands of French engineers. In this one they are building part of an aeroplane.

YOUNG PEOPLE

In 2010, one in four people between the ages of 16 and 25 was unemployed. The government is trying to help by paying employers to take on apprentices so young people can get skills and work experience.

Trade: buying and selling

France's most important trading partners are the United Kingdom, Germany, Spain, and Italy. France **imports** and **exports** machinery and equipment, cars, crude oil, aircraft, textiles, plastics, and chemicals.

France fared better than most large economies with the global **credit crunch** that began in 2008, but there were still job losses. Overall unemployment remains at 9.1 per cent, which is higher than the European average of 8.2 per cent.

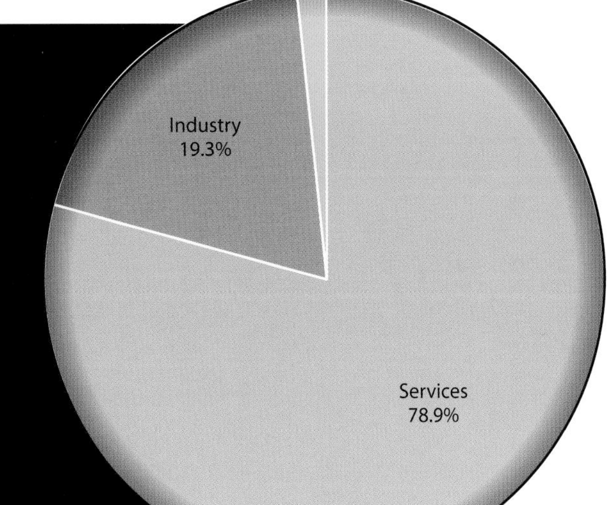

Gross Domestic Product (GDP) is the total amount of goods or services made in a country in a year. This pie chart shows what business types are important to the French economy, such as tourism. France is the most visited country in the world, with 75 million tourists every year.

Wildlife: protecting nature

France has large areas of relatively unspoilt **habitat** that supports a wide range of native wildlife.

High up in the rocky Alps lives the Alpine ibex. This wild goat can defend itself against predators such as wolves with its long, curved horns. In the early 20th century, the Alpine ibex was nearly hunted to **extinction**, but it is now protected by law.

Horses of the marsh

Camargue horses have lived wild in the marshes of the Camargue region in the south of France for thousands of years. The horses are small, sturdy, and tough. They are born brown or black and become white as they get older.

Camargue horses are protected and each new birth is registered.

The beautiful waterways and coast of the Calanques are due to become a national park in 2011.

Conservation success

The mountains of the Pyrenees in southwest France are home to the Pyrenean brown bear. The bear was hunted to near-extinction in the 1990s, but it was re-introduced in 1996 when three bears were brought from Slovenia. The bears have been **breeding** successfully, and there are now believed to be about 15 brown bears in the mountains.

National Parks

There are six national parks in mainland France, covering two per cent of the country and attracting over seven million visitors every year. Vanoise National Park in the Alps was created in 1963 and covers 528 square kilometres (204 square miles). It is free to enter national parks in France.

How to say...

cat	*le chat*	(luh sha)
dog	*le chien*	(luh she-ann)
wolf	*le loup*	(luh loo)
boar	*le sanglier*	(luh son-glee-eh)
rabbit	*le lapin*	(luh lap-an)
bird	*l'oiseau*	(lwa-zo)
horse	*le cheval*	(luh sheval)
eagle	*l'aigle*	(leg-la)
bear	*l'ours*	(lawss)

Environmental awareness

Like many **industrialized** countries, France has its share of environmental problems. Acid rain harms the country's forests while factories and vehicle **emissions** cause air pollution in the cities. In the countryside, agricultural chemicals such as fertilizers run off the fields and pollute rivers. Strict environmental protection laws are now in place. These aim to cut carbon emissions and limit water and air pollution.

Daily life

The French public are very aware of environmental issues. Most shops sell drinks in glass bottles that can be returned for refilling. Supermarkets charge for plastic bags so shoppers take their own reusable ones. All towns and cities have recycling bins for glass, paper, cans, and **landfill** waste.

Powering the nation

Most of France's electricity comes from nuclear power. There are 58 nuclear power plants all over the country. Nuclear power is clean to **generate**, but it produces highly **toxic** waste.

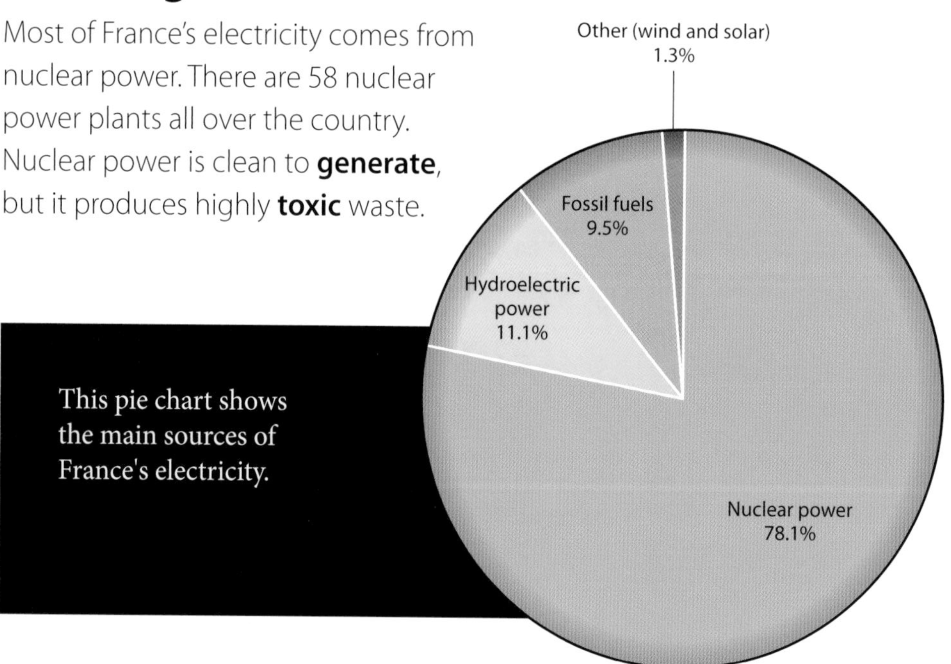

This pie chart shows the main sources of France's electricity.

Most of France's electricity comes from nuclear power stations.

How to say...

Earth	*la terre*	(la tair)
nature	*la nature*	(la na-teur)
the environment	*l'environnement*	(lon-veer-onnamon)
global warming	*le réchauffement climatique*	(luh ray-shorfmon kleemateek)
polluted water	*l'eau polluée*	(low pol-loo-way)
recycling	*le recyclage*	(luh re-seek-larg)
pollution	*la pollution*	(la polooshun)
green	*vert*	(vair)

Infrastructure: politics and people

The French parliament consists of two houses: the Senate with 348 **elected** members and the National Assembly with 577. Senators serve six-year terms whilst the National Assembly is elected every five years. The National Assembly meets at the Palais Bourbon in central Paris.

Political parties

The four main political parties are the Socialist party, the conservative Rassemblement pour la République, the Union pour la Democratie Française, and the French Communist party.

The president leads the government and he or she is **voted** in for a five-year term. The president then appoints the prime minister. The voting age is 18 in France.

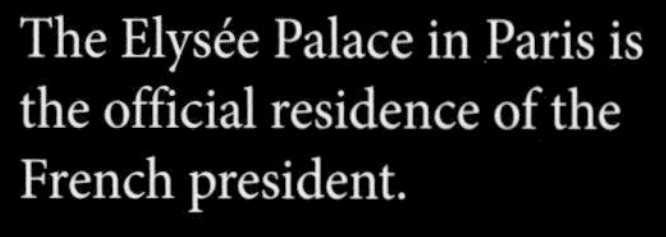

The Elysée Palace in Paris is the official residence of the French president.

Part of Europe

France is one of 27 countries in the **European Union (EU)**. The EU is a political and economic union with an elected parliament. There are many common **policies** across Europe dealing with **trade** and defence. EU law allows people to move, travel, and work easily in other member countries.

YOUNG PEOPLE

The European Youth Parliament (EYP) has many different committees across Europe including one in France. The EYP offers young people aged between 16 and 22 a chance to express their opinions on political and topical issues. Students are encouraged to debate, think independently, and find solutions to problems.

Healthcare

When French people are ill, they go to the doctor. They pay for the consultation and claim the costs back on their **health insurance**. French employees pay about 20 per cent of their salary to fund the **social security system**. The World Health Organization (WHO) ranks France's healthcare system as the world's best.

France is divided into different regions. Each region has a regional capital city.

Getting around

France has some challenging land for road builders and engineers. The Alps and Pyrenees have many tunnels through the mountains as well as zig-zagging roads up to the high ski resorts.

Autoroutes are the motorways that cross the country, mainly from north to south. To travel on most of these, people pay a toll. The cost depends on how far the driver has travelled. In France, cars drive on the right.

Beating the traffic

In Paris and other large cities, such as Lyon and Marseille, there is a Metro (underground) system. The Metro helps to prevent traffic jams and reduce air pollution. In Paris, many people use the *bateau-bus* (boat-bus) that travels to different stops along the River Seine.

Daily life

Traffic jams in Paris have been eased by a bicycle hire scheme. There are *vélib* stations (short for *vélo-libre* or "bike freedom") all over the city with more than 20,000 bikes in use. Cyclists pay for the time they use the bike and can return the bike to any station.

It takes 2 hours 15 minutes to travel the 495 kilometres (307 miles) from Paris to London on the Eurostar. The trains go under the sea in a tunnel and travel at 300 kmh (186 mph).

At 343 metres (1,125 feet), the Millau Viaduct is the world's tallest vehicle bridge. The Eiffel Tower could fit underneath it!

Transport in France	
Railways	32,175 kilometres
Roads	894,000 kilometres
Canals	8,500 kilometres
Number of airports	41 (of any major size)
Number of private cars	469 per 1,000 people

Waterways

All over France, rivers and canals are used to transport industrial goods by barge. The main rivers are the Rhone, the Seine, the Garonne, and the Loire. The main canals are the Canal de Bourgogne, the Canal du Rhin au Rhone, and the Canal de la Marne au Rhin.

School life

Nearly all children in France attend schools funded by the government. Lessons begin at 8.30 a.m. and finish around 4.30 p.m. There is no school on Wednesday afternoons because children play sport or have music lessons then. Many schools have lessons on Saturday mornings.

School is **compulsory** between the ages of six and sixteen. Children learn French, history, geography, social studies, maths, science, art, and music. Children also learn English or another foreign language.

How to say...

French	*le français*	(luh fronsay)
English	*l'anglais*	(long-glay)
social studies	*les sciences sociales*	(lay sea-ons so-see-arl)
art	*l'art*	(lar)
chemistry	*la chimie*	(la shimee)
history	*l'histoire*	(listwah)
geography	*la géo(graphie)*	(la jayograffie)
maths	*les mathématiques*	(lay mat-eh-mateek)
music	*la musique*	(la moozeek)

Daily life

The school lunch break lasts for two hours. Pupils go home to eat with their families or eat in the school canteen. Lunch always has three courses: salad or soup, a main course, and then cheese or dessert.

French children don't wear school uniform.

Higher education

After primary school, pupils go to a *collége* from the age of 11 to 15 and then go on to a *lycée*. Students can leave school at 16 to find work or they can stay until they are 18 and study for the *baccalauréate* exam to go to university. French universities have high standards and many students come to study from other French-speaking nations.

Culture: art, music, and leisure

French **culture** is associated with style, from the art museums and fashion catwalks of Paris, to the glamorous Cannes Film Festival.

Capital of culture

Paris has more than 70 museums, famous landmarks like the Eiffel Tower and Notre Dame cathedral, and thousands of cafés. The Musée d'Orsay has a large collection of paintings by the Impressionists.

THE IMPRESSIONISTS

In the late 19th century, a new style of painting began. Impressionist painters studied the effect that light had on their subjects and they then tried to paint it. Claude Monet, Berthe Morisot, and Auguste Renoir are famous Impressionists.

Sitting in a café is part of daily life in Paris.

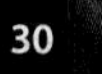

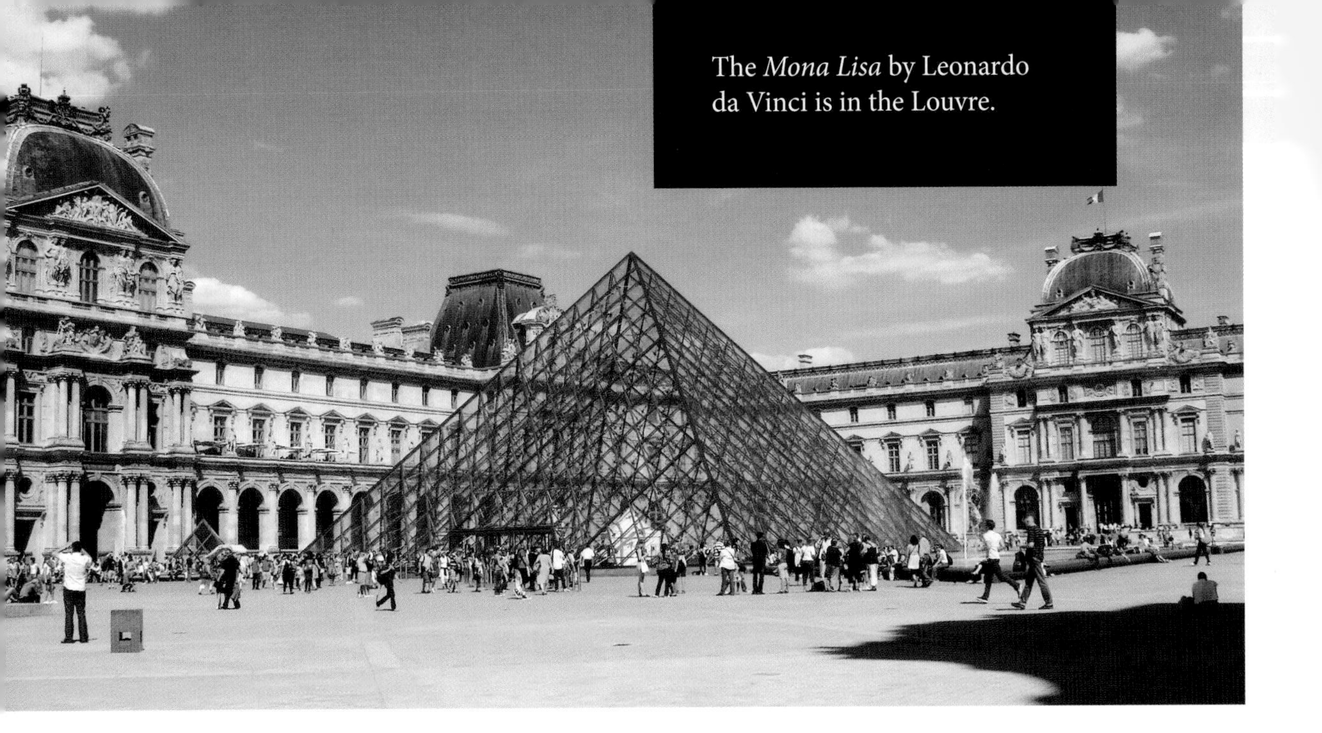

The *Mona Lisa* by Leonardo da Vinci is in the Louvre.

Musical figures

France has produced many **classical** composers, such as Claude Debussy who wrote "Clair de Lune" and Camille Saint-Saëns who wrote *The Carnival of the Animals*. Other popular French musicians include the nightclub singer, Edith Piaf.

EDITH PIAF (1915–1963)

Edith Piaf was known as the "little sparrow" because she was only 142 centimetres (4 feet 7 inches) tall. Her songs reflected her experiences. Her most famous song is "Je ne regrette rien", which means "I regret nothing".

Book club

France has a great tradition of literature. Emile Zola and Gustave Flaubert wrote about people's lives and their problems. Molière wrote comic plays poking fun at the upper classes and Alexandre Dumas created swashbuckling heroes such as the three Musketeers.

Lights, camera, action!

In 1895 the Lumière brothers invented the portable film camera and cinema was born. The French film industry has been making successful films for over 100 years. In 2008, Marion Cotillard won an Oscar for playing Edith Piaf in *La Vie en Rose*. Every year, film stars from around the world attend the Cannes Film Festival and compete to win the Palme d'Or prize for best film.

FRENCH AUTHORS

French writers have written many classic children's stories. *The Little Prince* by Antoine de Saint Exupéry and *Babar the Elephant* by Jean de Brunhoff have been translated into many languages. The most famous stories are by Charles Perrault who was one of the first to publish fairy tales. "Sleeping Beauty", "Cinderella", and "Little Red Riding Hood" are loved by children all over the world.

National holidays

By law, every French **citizen** can take five weeks of annual holiday. On top of this, there are 11 national holidays each year including Bastille Day. Lots of banks, shops, and museums close on these days.

Sporting nation

Popular sports in France include rugby, football, tennis, and **boules**. Climbing, hiking, and skiing are popular in the mountains.

The Tour de France is one of the biggest annual sporting events in the world. International teams of cyclists pedal over 3,600 kilometres (2,237 miles) around the country in three weeks, riding up huge mountains in the Alps and the Pyrenees. The race always finishes in Paris.

Festival food

French fries and French toast are well known, but what about snails in garlic butter and lightly fried frogs' legs? These **delicacies** are eaten as special treats, usually at Christmas.

French crèpes

Ask an adult to help you make this delicious treat.

Ingredients

- 235 grams plain flour
- 1 teaspoon white sugar
- ¼ teaspoon salt
- 3 eggs
- 475 millilitres milk
- 2 tablespoons butter, melted
- sugar and lemon juice to serve

What to do

1. Sift together the flour, sugar, and salt in a bowl.
2. In a different bowl, beat the eggs and milk together.
3. Add the flour mixture to the eggs and stir in the melted butter to make a batter.
4. Heat a lightly oiled frying pan over medium-high heat.
5. Pour 2 tablespoons of batter into the pan for each crèpe.
6. Tip and turn the pan to spread the batter as thinly as possible. Brown on both sides.
7. Serve hot with sugar and lemon juice.

France today

France is a country that captures the imagination. From the romance of Paris to the splendour of its **chateaux**, the country's artistic **culture** has produced writers and artists who have made their mark on the world. The country's historic buildings, food, and spectacular landscape ensure that millions of people visit each year.

Modern life

France today has a vibrant **multicultural** society with a strong sense of its own history and pride in its traditions. Many people from its former **colonies** come to live and work in France, adding to the cultural mix.

YOUNG PEOPLE

French teenagers like to keep up with the latest electronic gadgets. It is fashionable to have a *téléphone portable* (mobile phone), a *baladeur* (MP3 player), and an *ordinateur portable* (laptop). They also *surfer l'Internet*. There are cyber cafés in most towns, as only 52 per cent of French homes have Internet access.

Political progression

France is taking a lead within European politics and on the global stage. As a permanent member of the **United Nations' Security Council**, France works closely with other countries to find solutions to international problems, such as war and terrorism.

The future

France is a country that doesn't stand still. It's always changing and developing in order to improve the quality of life for its **citizens**. It's a country that embraces new technology and design. However, French history, language, and identity remain very important to its people as the country moves into the future.

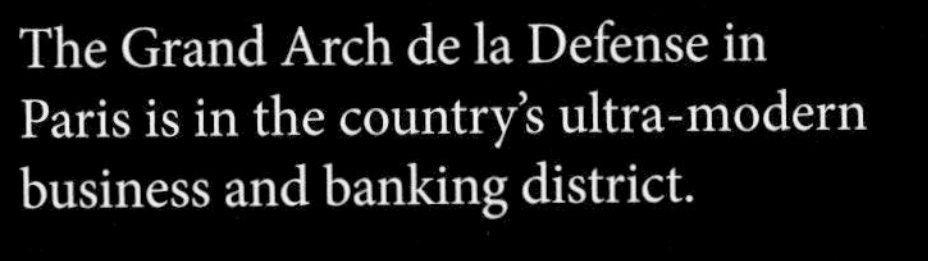

The Grand Arch de la Defense in
Paris is in the country's ultra-modern
business and banking district.

Fact file

Official language: French

Capital city: Paris

Bordering countries: Andorra, Belgium, Germany, Italy, Luxembourg, Monaco, Spain, Switzerland

Population: 64 million (2 million overseas)

Largest cities in terms of population: Paris, Lyon, Marseille

Life expectancy at birth: 77.91 years for men; 84.44 years for women

Religions: **Roman Catholic**: up to 88%, **Protestant**: 2%, Jewish: 1%, Muslim: up to 10%, other/none: 4%

National flower: lily (fleur de lys)

Area: 551,500 square kilometres (212,935 square miles)

Major rivers: Seine, Somme, Rhône, Garonne, Loire

Highest point: Mont Blanc in the Alps at 4,810 metres (15,780 feet)

Currency: euro (100 cents = 1 euro)

Natural resources: coal, iron ore, uranium, arsenic, timber, fish

Imports: machinery and equipment, vehicles, crude oil, aircraft, plastics, chemicals

Exports: machinery and transportation equipment, aircraft, plastics, chemicals, pharmaceutical products, iron and steel, beverages

Major industries: aerospace engineering, chemicals, tourism

Literacy rates: 99 per cent of the population can read and write

Climate: temperate continental

Membership of international organizations: **G8**, UN Security Council, **European Union**, eurozone

Units of measurement: metric

World Heritage Sites:	32 **World Heritage Sites** including Palace of Versailles, bridge of Avignon, banks of the Seine in Paris, Notre Dame cathedral, Loire valley chateaux
Famous inventions:	Braille (1824), aspirin (1853)
Other territories administered by France:	Martinique, Guadeloupe, French Guiana, Réunion. There are 29 countries and regions around the world that have French as an official language, including the Canadian province of Quebec, Algeria, Madagascar, Cameroon, and Vietnam.
Festivals:	Cannes Film Festival, the Menton lemon festival, the Paris Chocolate Show, Dijon's November food and wine fair
Famous French people:	Thierry Henry (footballer), Richard Gasquet (tennis player), Montgolfier brothers (inventors), Lumière brothers (inventors), Claude Debussy (composer), Louis Pasteur (scientist), Berthe Morisot (artist), Claude Monet (artist), Victor Hugo (writer), Pierre Curie (scientist), Coco Chanel (designer), Brigitte Bardot (actor), Gérard Depardieu (actor)

French national anthem

The French National Anthem is called "La Marseillaise". It was written in 1792 by Claude Joseph Rouget de Lisle and was a revolutionary song to encourage the working classes to rise up against the **nobles**. This is the first verse:

Allons, enfants de la patrie,	*Come, children of the Fatherland,*
Le jour de gloire est arrivé.	*The day of glory has arrived!*
Contre nous, de la tyrannie,	*Against us,* ***Tyranny****'s*
L'étendard sanglant est levé;	*Bloody banner is raised,*
l'étendard sanglant est levé.	*Do you hear in the countryside*
Entendez-vous, dans les campagnes	*Those ferocious soldiers roaring?*
Mugir ces féroces soldats?	*They come up to your arms*
Ils viennent jusque dans nos bras	*to cut the throats of our sons,*
Égorger nos fils, nos compagnes.	*our comrades.*
Aux armes, citoyens!	*To arms, citizens!*

Timeline

AD is short for *Anno Domini*, which is Latin for "in the year of our Lord". AD is added before a date and means that the date occurred after the birth of Jesus Christ, for example, AD 720.

1st–5th century AD	The region of Gaul (roughly the same area as modern France) is settled mainly by the Gauls, Celts, and Franks, and is under Roman rule
AD 486	Clovis I, leader of the Franks, conquers northern and central France. **Roman Catholicism** is adopted.
AD 771	Charlemagne (Charles the Great) unites more areas of France, as well as parts of northern Italy, Germany, and Spain
1066	William of Normandy invades England and takes the throne
around 1337	Edward III of England claims the French crown Beginning of the Hundred Years' War
1415	Battle of Agincourt. Henry V of England defeats French forces.
1558	Calais returns to French control, marking the end of English rule in France
1572	St Bartholomew's Day **Massacre**
1598	**Edict** of Nantes means religious freedom for all
1635	Académie Française created
1643–1715	Reign of Louis XIV. France is the dominant power in Europe.
1682	Louis XIV establishes the royal court at the Palace of Versailles
1789	French Revolution
1792	National anthem, "La Marseillaise", is written
1799	Napoleon takes power
1803–14	Napoleon expands the French **Empire**
1804	Napoleon crowns himself Emperor
1809	The baccalauréate exam is created
1814	Napoleon is **exiled** to Elba

1815	Napoleon returns and is defeated at the Battle of Waterloo
1830–1848	Reign of Louis–Philippe
1889	Eiffel Tower is built
1895	Lumière brothers invent the portable film camera
1903	First Tour de France takes place
1914–1918	World War I takes place
1939	Start of World War II
22 June 1940	France surrenders to Nazi Germany. German occupation of France begins. The **Resistance** tries to disrupt German rule.
1944	France is freed from German occupation
1945	End of World War II
1946	First Cannes Film Festival
1979	European Parliament opens
1993	**European Union** is formed to ease **trade** and business between member states
1994	The Channel Tunnel opens and Eurostar trains start running between Paris and London
1998	France hosts and wins the World Cup
1 January 1999	France adopts the euro as its **currency**
2008	Marion Cotillard wins an Oscar for playing Edith Piaf in *La Vie en Rose*
2007–2010	The global **credit crunch** creates high youth unemployment in France

Glossary

amputation surgical removal of a limb

boules popular ball game like bowls

breed bear offspring; a word usually used for animals or birds

chateau (plural: chateaux) castle or large house

citizen legal resident of a country

classical serious, artistic music, often played by an orchestra or piano

colony country ruled from afar by another country

compulsory required by rules or law

credit crunch global economic problem caused when the cash flow or credit from banks stops and many businesses cannot get loans. This results in mass unemployment.

culture practices, traditions, and beliefs of a society

currency banknotes and coins accepted in exchange for goods and services

delicacy food which is expensive, hard to get, and highly thought of

dialect regional language

dormant not active or erupting

dubbed when a new soundtrack is added to a film or TV programme, usually in a different language

economy to do with money and the industry and jobs in a country

edict official order

elect choose by voting. The public elects a person to represent them in Parliament.

emissions gases released into the atmosphere from factories and homes

empire group of countries ruled by a single powerful country

European Union (EU) political and economic union of (currently) 27 European countries

exiled sent away and banned from your home country

export sell goods to another country

extinction dying out of a species

extravagance over the top spending or indulgence

G8 group of the eight richest countries in the world

generate produce

genius extremely clever person

guillotine device used to behead people

habitat environment where a plant or animal is found

health insurance money paid in advance for health protection

import buy goods from another country

industrialized well-developed production methods

landfill rubbish that is buried under ground in large areas called landfill sites

massacre deliberate killing of many people

monarch king or queen

multicultural mix of people from different cultures and countries

noble person belonging to a high and powerful social class

policy idea and course of action

power vacuum political situation created when there is no clear leader

Protestant Christian who practises their faith and doesn't follow the pope's leadership

republic country with an elected leader and no monarch

Resistance French freedom organization whose members fought against German occupation during Wolrd War II

resource means available for a country to develop, such as minerals and energy sources

Roman Catholic Christian who follows the beliefs of the Roman Catholic Church and the leadership of the pope

sniper marksman, sharpshooter

social security system government system of welfare ensuring that financial help is given to people in need

tax money paid by people to the government. Taxes can come from wages or be placed on goods that people buy.

toxic poisonous, extremely harmful to health

trade buying and selling of goods, usually between countries

trench long narrow ditch in the ground used as shelter from enemy fire or attack

trench foot common problem for soldiers during World War I, caused by living in wet and cold trenches. Limited blood circulation to the foot results in decay.

tribe independent social group, historically often made up of primitive or nomadic people

tyranny very harsh, strict government

United Nations' Security Council international committee of the world's most powerful nations devoted to maintaining world peace

vote choose. People vote for someone to win an election.

World Heritage Site special site of global importance

Find out more

Books

Festivals and Food: France, Teresa Fisher (Wayland, 2006)
France (Country Files), Celia Tidmarsh (Franklin Watts, 2005)
French for Children (Language for Children), Catherine Bruzzone, (McGraw-Hill Professional, 2003)
Horrible Histories: France, Terry Deary and Martin Brown (Scholastic, 2011)
You Wouldn't Want to Be an Aristocrat in the French Revolution!: A Horrible Time in Paris You'd Rather Avoid, Jim Pipe (Children's Press, 2007)

Websites

en.chateauversailles.fr/history-
Go to the Palace of Versailles website to learn more about the history of the French kings and queens, and where they lived.

us.franceguide.com
Visit the official website of the French Government Tourist office, to find out more about the different regions of France, things to do, and places to see.

www.bbc.co.uk/schools/primaryfrench
This website has interactive games and activities to help you learn French.

Places to visit

If you ever get the chance to go to France, here are some of the places you could visit:

Arc de Triomphe, Paris
Climb to the top of Napoleon's triumphal arch and look down the Champs-Elysées to the Louvre.

Caves de Niaux, Ariège
See prehistoric cave paintings and impressive rock formations in some of Europe's largest underground caverns.

Champs-Elysées, Paris
Walk up the grandest avenue in the capital.

Eiffel Tower, Paris
Walk to the first level or ride to the top to get fabulous views of Paris.

Futuroscope Park, Poitiers
Have fun at France's largest interactive science and technology park.

Louvre Museum, Paris
Explore this world-famous art museum and see the Mona Lisa.

Luberon Valley, Provence
See beautiful hilltop villages surrounded by fields of sunflowers and lavender.

Mer de Glace railway and Aiguille du midi cable car, Chamonix
Since 1908, a train service has been taking tourists up to the incredible Mer de Glace glacier. After that, go 3,800 metres (12,467 feet) to the top of the Alps and see Mont Blanc up close!

Musee d'Orsay, Paris
See the large collection of Impressionist paintings at this museum.

Palace of Versailles, near Paris
Visit the home of the kings and queens of France and see the luxury in which they lived.

Tuillerie Gardens, Paris
Hang out with the locals in the capital's most central park.

Topic tools

You can use these topic tools for your school projects. Trace the map onto a sheet of paper, using the thick black outline to guide you.

The French flag is called the *Tricolore*, or "three colours". It's easy to see why! Copy the flag design and then colour in your picture. Make sure you use the right colours.

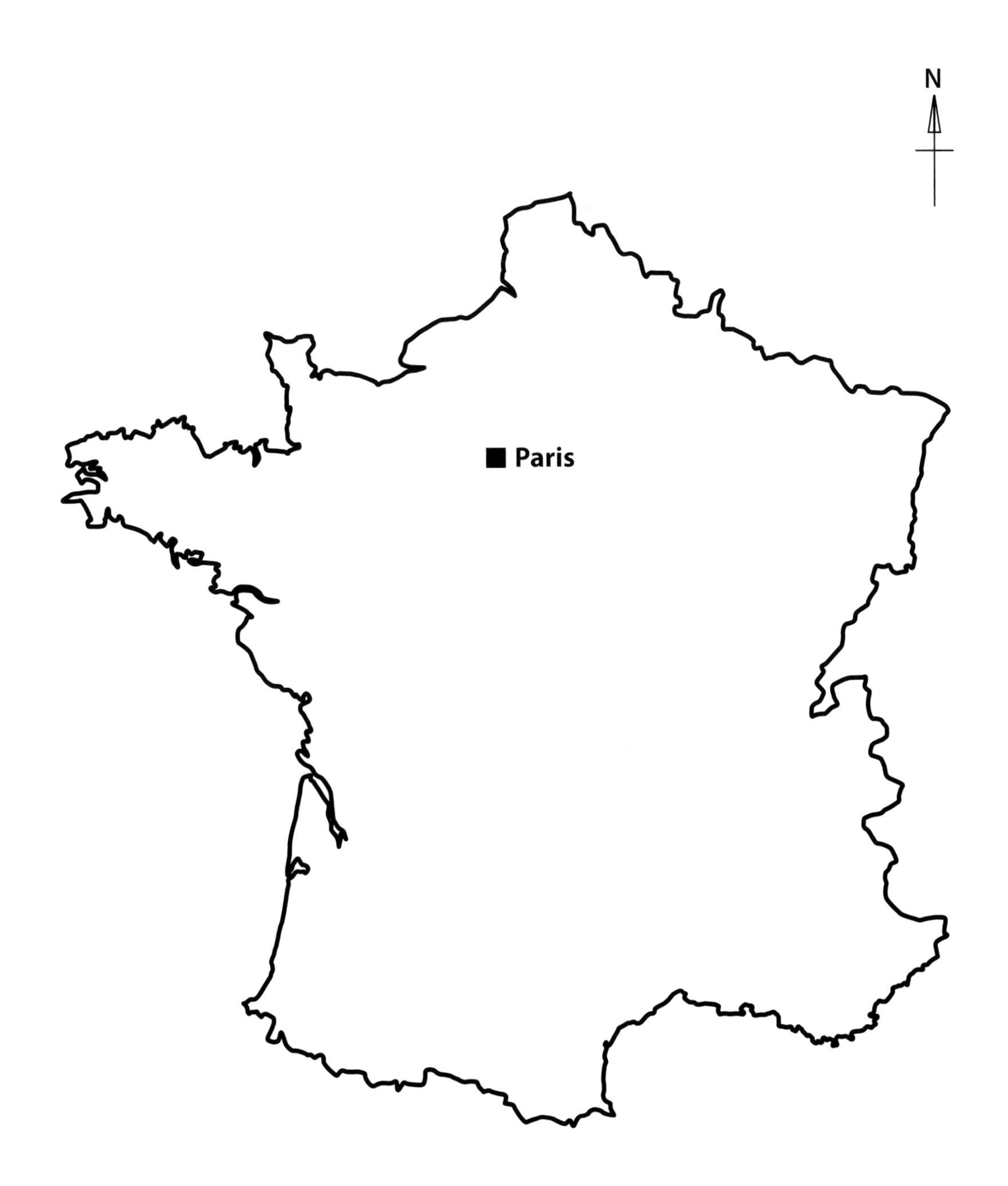
N
Paris

Index

Titles in the series

Afghanistan	978 1 406 22778 9
Brazil	978 1 406 22785 7
Chile	978 1 406 22786 4
Costa Rica	978 1 406 22787 1
Cuba	978 1 406 22788 8
Czech Republic	978 1 406 22792 5
England	978 1 406 22799 4
Estonia	978 1 406 22793 2
France	978 1 406 22800 7
Germany	978 1 406 22801 4
Haiti	978 1 406 22789 5
Hungary	978 1 406 22794 9
India	978 1 406 22779 6
Iran	978 1 406 22780 2
Iraq	978 1 406 22781 9
Italy	978 1 406 22802 1
Latvia	978 1 406 22795 6
Lithuania	978 1 406 22796 3
Mexico	978 1 406 22790 1
Pakistan	978 1 406 22782 6
Poland	978 1 406 22797 0
Scotland	978 1 406 22803 8
Wales	978 1 406 22804 5
Yemen	978 1 406 22783 3

THE DOLL'S HOUSE DECORATOR

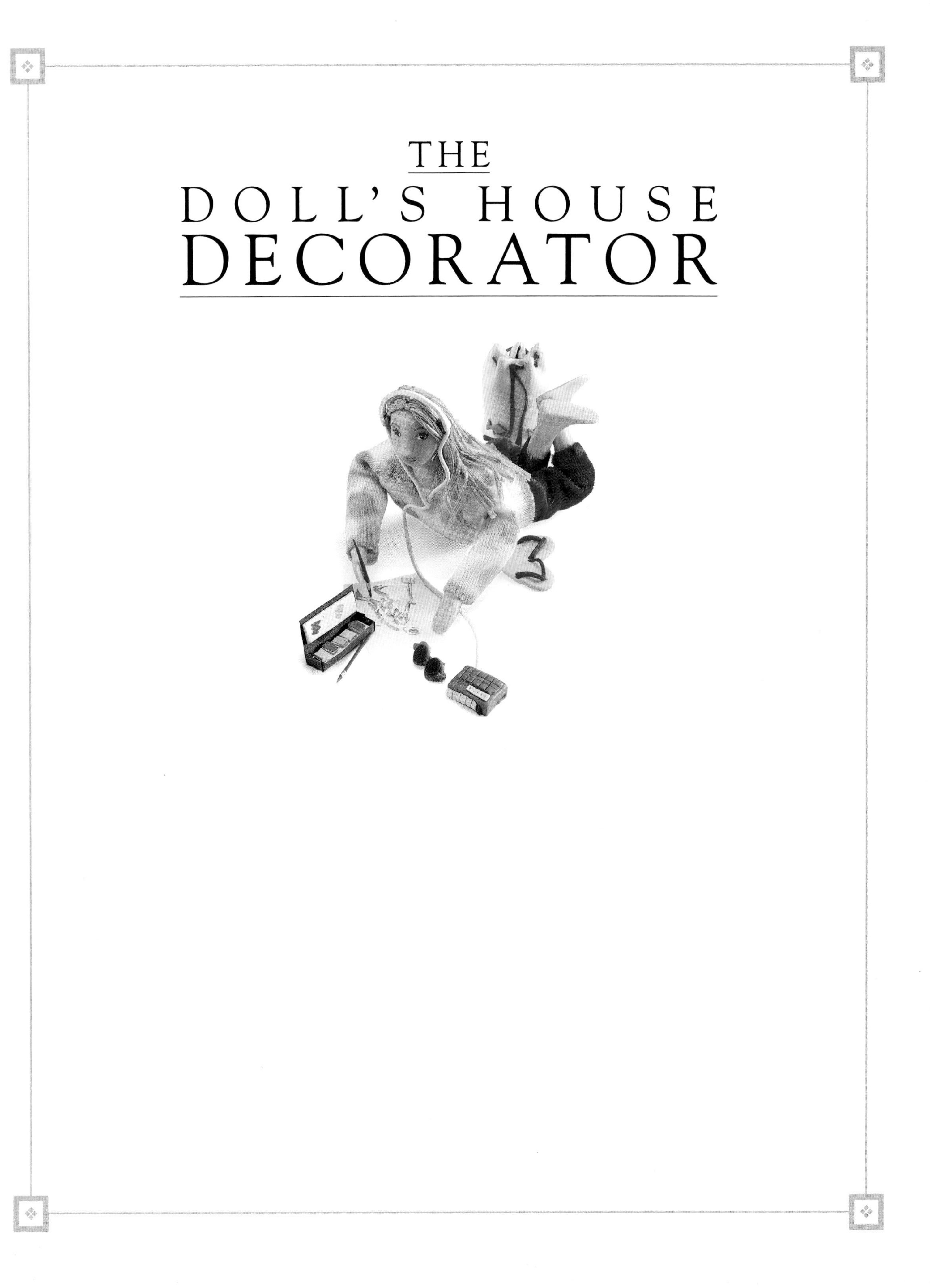

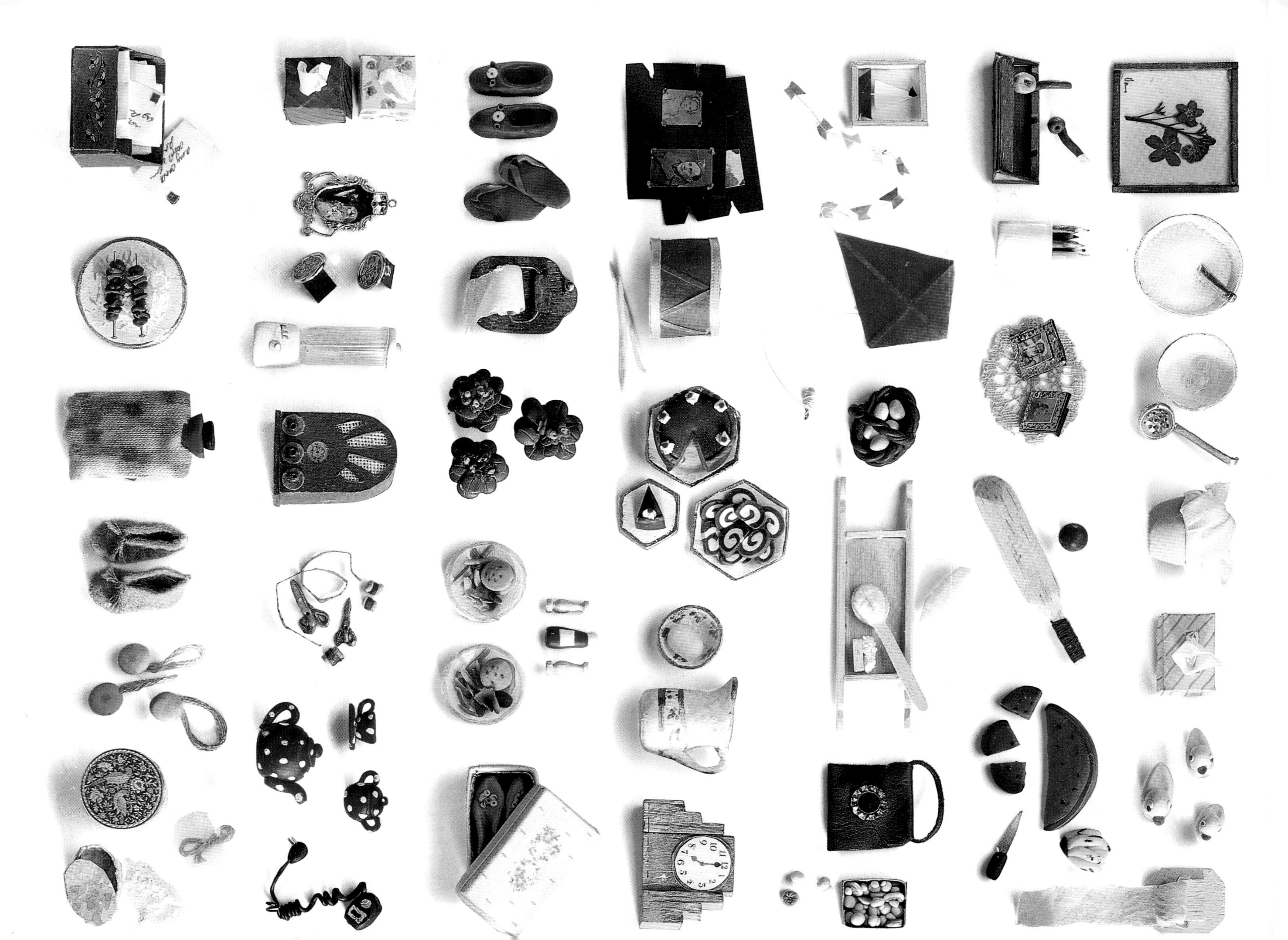

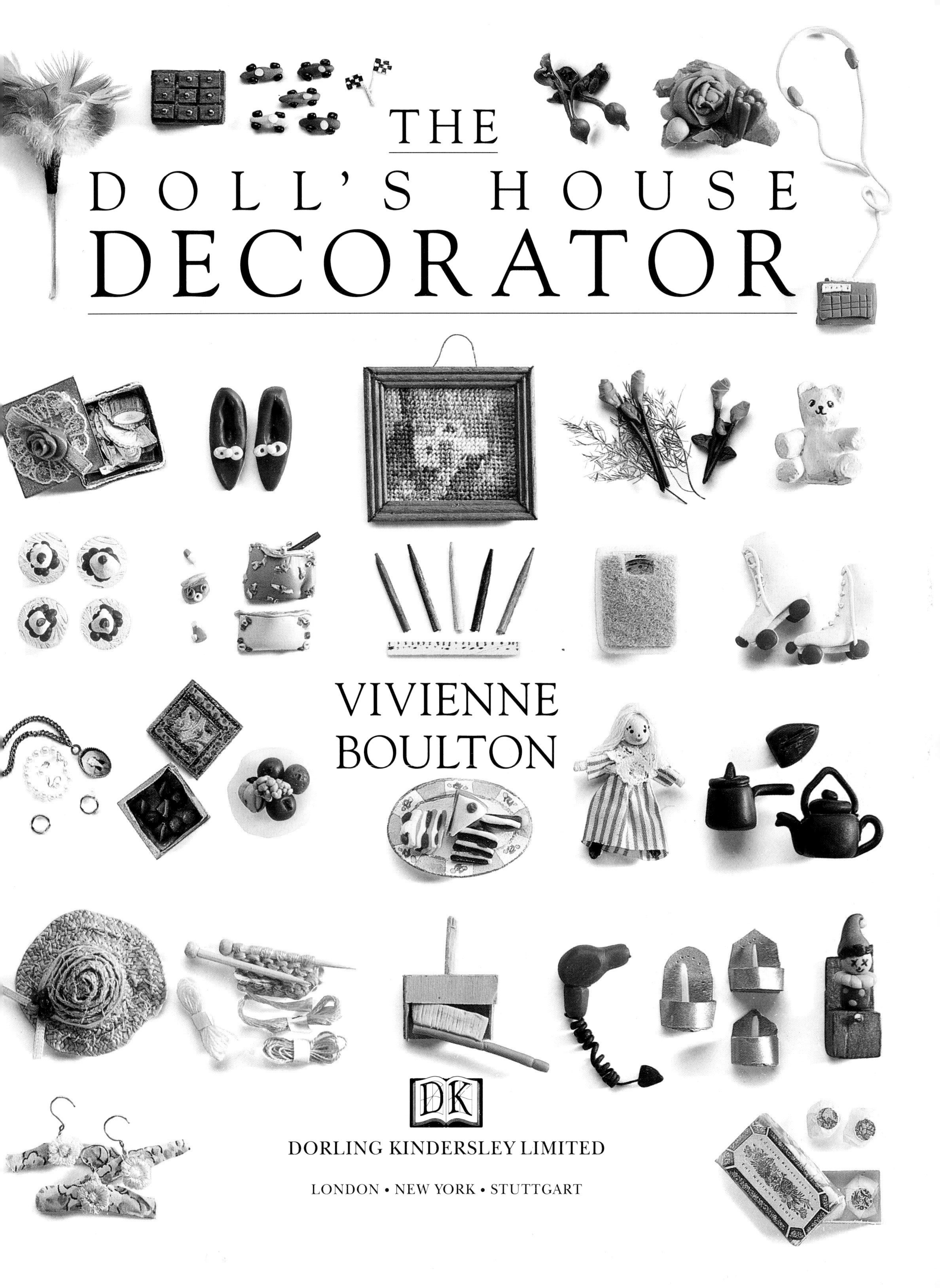

THE DOLL'S HOUSE DECORATOR

VIVIENNE BOULTON

DK

DORLING KINDERSLEY LIMITED

LONDON • NEW YORK • STUTTGART

Dedicated to Ella Waters, my grandmother

The Doll's House Decorator
is a
CARROLL & BROWN
original creation

Art Direction
Denise Brown Lyndel Donaldson

Editorial
Amy Carroll

Photography
David Murray Jules Selmes

Production Consultant
Lorraine Baird

Typesetting
Rowena Feeny

First published in Great Britain in 1992 by
Dorling Kindersley Limited
9 Henrietta Street, London WC2E 8PS

A CIP catalogue record for this book is available from the British Library.

ISBN 0-7513-0000-4

Reproduced by Colourscan, Singapore
Printed in Singapore by Tien Wah Press

Contents

INTRODUCTION

Welcome to a world of doll's house decoration that uses only readily available, inexpensive materials. Peruse the pages of this book and you will find a multitude of useful and attractive items to suit every doll's taste and needs. Though its scale may be small, the range of doll's house furnishings that can be created is limited only by your imagination.

Doll's house decoration as practised in this book depends upon the mastery of a few simple techniques applied to materials that are inexpensive and easy to acquire. Furniture for the most part is made of wood strip and cardboard, while smaller accessories are created from clay and plastic modelling materials. Paper and fabric, too, are essential for many household items and soft furnishings.

Immediately following this introduction is a section on the materials and techniques required for doll's house decorating. Not only will you learn how to transform plain card and wood into elaborately finished furnishings but you will begin to see how buttons, beads, and found objects can be transmuted into picture frames, bottles, and feather dusters. Soon practically everything you see will acquire decorative possibilities.

A doll's house can be decorated in any period style but the Victorian era is popular with the majority of dolls' house owners, and its rather overstuffed look provides scope for an enormous number of items. So although most of the rooms inside relate to Victorian times, several other styles are represented including Colonial, Art Deco, Country, and Contemporary.

All the major rooms in a house have been considered. There are kitchens, bedrooms – for adults and children, sitting rooms, and bathrooms.

Each one can be recreated to fit your doll's house or even a decorated box. As well as the furniture, each room comes complete with furnishings, accessories, decorative items, and the normal paraphernalia of everyday life – then and now. Everything has play value, too, and a selection of small items can provide a child with hours of creative activity – both in the making and in the using.

Selected items of furniture are photographed separately and come with full making-up instructions and templates. Tables, chairs, beds, wardrobes, cupboards, and washstands are among the items covered. Their instructions and templates are found in the back of the book. Templates should never be cut out but should always be traced over and transferred to the recommended materials.

Other pieces of furniture are variations of the major items and for them, extended captions give making-up directions and, if necessary, advice on adapting particular templates.

Most of the smaller items contained in the rooms are displayed on catalogue pages. Here you get to see hundreds of items up close, and are given instructions on how they are made. The range of accessories is enormous and includes crockery, cookware, food, clothing, soft furnishings, wall decorations, toys, jewellery, paper goods, linens, plants, boxes, and books.

Finally, a doll's house must be a home. Whose home it is falls within the abilities of a doll's house decorator– particularly as complete how-to instructions on creating and clothing the family of your choice are included. Again, a few simple materials can bring to life a cast of thousands.

So be prepared to be entertained, astonished, and inspired. Let the doll's house decorating begin!

WORKING WITH PAPER AND CARD

Paper products are the most versatile and widely available of all craft materials. Every kind of paper and paper product is useable – from specially constructed art board through to wrapping paper, printed illustrations, decorative boxes, tissue paper, and toilet paper! Start saving your scraps; they are certain to be put to good use.

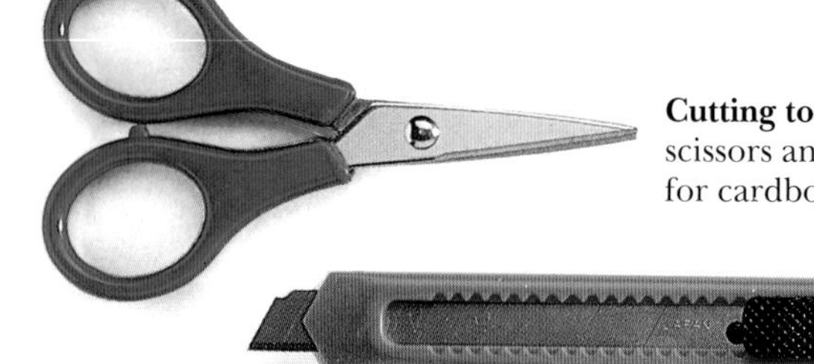

Cutting tools include scissors and a craft knife for cardboard

Glue should be an all-purpose clear, strong adhesive; glue sticks are handy also

Sugar paper (centre and right) can be effective as picture mounts, blotters and book jackets

Foil (left) is used for "mirrors" and gift wrapping. It can be bought in sheets or as adhesive-backed plastic, or taken from sweet wrappers and wine bottles. Kitchen foil can be used also

Shapes and rulers are useful for creating curved and geometric items

Wrapping paper is used to cover walls and boxes

Tissue paper is used as the real thing and for creating fires

Masking tape is used to roughly assemble pieces, and for hinges and plants

Tape is used for joins; transparent tape is handy when an invisible join is wanted

Cardboard is a thick card that is used for constructing many of the pieces of furniture

Card is thinner and is used for backings and many of the smaller accessories

How to make an
ORNAMENTAL FERN

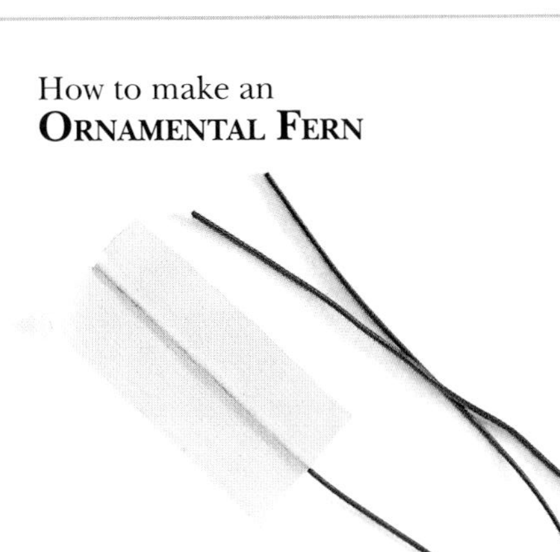

1 ~ Cut a length of green garden wire and cover two-thirds of both sides with a 2.5 cm (1 in) wide masking-tape strip.

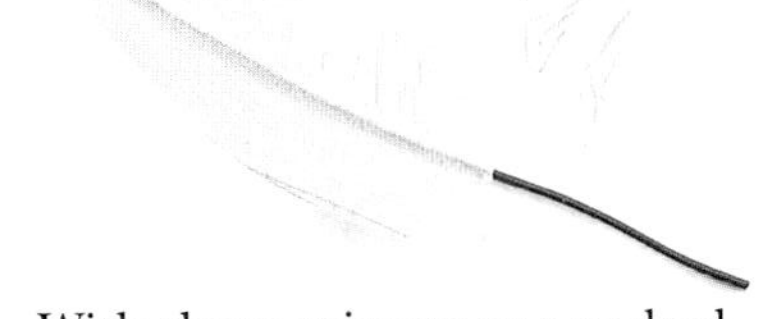

2 ~ With sharp scissors or a scalpel cut leaf shapes, removing some tape from in-between each leaf.

3 ~ Paint leaves with green acrylic paint. Group together at least six leaves and "plant" in a wad of self-hardening clay in a terracotta pot made of self-hardening clay. Water with care. Plants prefer a sunny exposure, and look effective in bathrooms and sitting rooms.

How to make a
HAT BOX

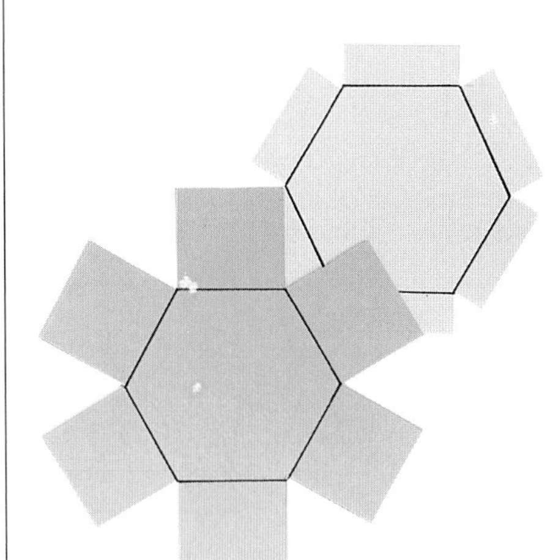

1 ~ From cardboard cut out appropriately-sized circles for the box and its lid, and mark the central hexagons. Cut away "v" shapes as shown.

2 ~ Using a straight edge and scissors, score along the hexagon lines. Very carefully, with your fingers, bend the sides into the middle.

3 ~ Use pieces of masking tape to reinforce the corners of the box and its lid.

4 ~ Cover box with gift-wrap paper using a glue stick.

5 ~ Complete decoration with ribbon and flower trim as desired.

Useful Paper Items

A large variety of readily available paper products serve a multitude of functions in the doll's house.

Stamps and illustrations from magazines and catalogues are ideal for pictures, children's games, scrap books, collections, and fire screens

Transfers, metallic strips, and gold stars can be used to provide ornamental detail on furniture and furnishings

Sweet wrappers, particularly cellophane ones, can be used as decoration for boxes and jars and for gift wrapping

Working with Clay/Modelling Medium

There are two major types of modelling material used in this book. One is a plastic medium, most often sold as Fimo, which needs to be baked to harden. The other preferred type is a self-hardening clay sold as Das.

Modelling medium comes in many colours and several textures so further painting is not normally required and it is good for recreating specialist "china" effects. Use a felt-tip pen to roll it out, so the medium won't adhere to its nonstick surface. To make it malleable for use, warm it in your hands. Because of its many colours it is ideal for creating food – everything from soup to nuts.

Self-hardening clay is more malleable to begin with but it only comes in neutral and terracotta. It can be softened with occasional sprays of water if it hardens prematurely. Before painting with an acrylic primer and acrylic or water-based paints, it needs to dry out for about 12 to 24 hours. This material is ideal for crockery that requires fine decoration or for anything with a handle.

Modelling tools can help work small amounts of clay

Rolling pin is ideal for working large, flat amounts of modelling materials

Glue should be strong, all-purpose clear adhesive

Craft knife for cutting media

Modelling medium comes in a variety of shades

Water spray can be used for softening self-hardening clay

Greaseproof paper provides a nonstick surface when rolling out clay

Self-hardening clay comes in only two shades

How to make a **PITCHER**

1 ~ Roll clay to form a cylinder shape. Pinch and press cylinder to form a lip, flat top, waist, and bulbous base. Let dry.

2 ~ Sand to smooth away any rough edges.

3 ~ Roll a long sausage shape for the handle. Spray pitcher to dampen and attach top end of handle, pressing gently.

4 ~ Then bring down other end, curving it gently, and press to attach. Neaten, if necessary, with scalpel.

5 ~ When pitcher is dry, sand gently. If handle falls off, it can be reattached with glue.

6 ~ Paint with primer and acrylic or water-based paints.

Sandpaper

Essential for producing a fine finish, particularly on large items such as the bathroom suite (see page 44), sandpaper comes in a number of grades. Start with coarse grade then apply finer sheets.

Colour is not an indication of grain

Emery boards or small pieces of sandpaper, wrapped around a pencil or small block of wood, create ideal tools for refining small areas on modelled items

How to make a **STRAWBERRY SHORTCAKE**

1 ~ Roll out "pastry" and "cream" using tan and white modelling media; cut into strips. Make "berries".

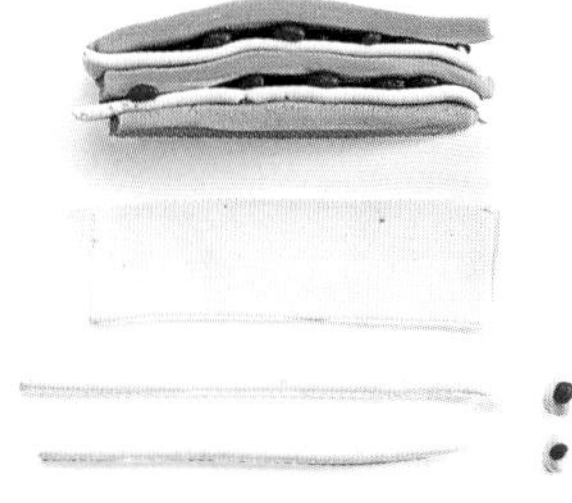

2 ~ With pastry on bottom, cover with cream and strawberries. Repeat to form two layers.

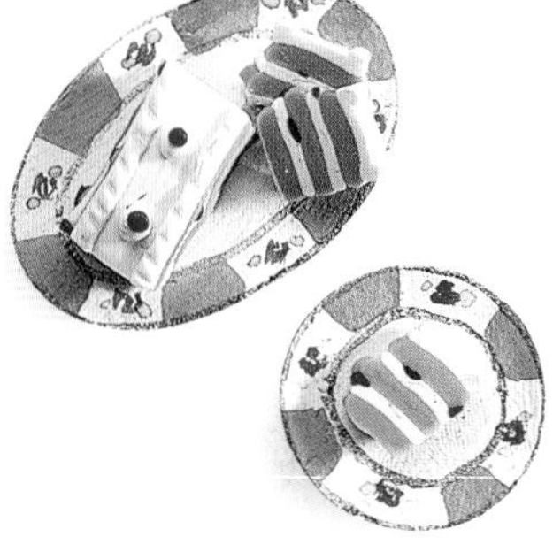

3 ~ After baking, neaten edges with a sharp knife then cut into "slices" for serving.

How to make a **CAULIFLOWER**

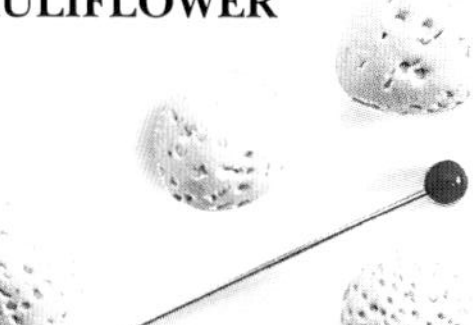

1 ~ With white modelling medium make the "head". Use a pin to pick out the curds.

2 ~ Press balls of green modelling medium, between finger and thumb. Curl the "leaves" in at the edges.

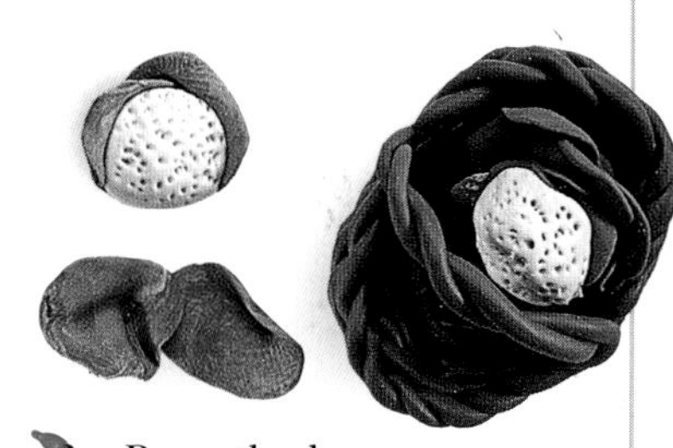

3 ~ Press the leaves against the head, overlapping them at the back until the cauliflower is complete.

How to make a **PLATE**

1 ~ Roll out clay on greaseproof paper so it is 3mm ($^1/_8$ in) thick. With knife, roughly cut out shape – a square approximately 38 mm ($1^1/_2$ in).

2 ~ With large pen top or other suitable cylinder, press into middle of square; the edges will lift. Raise the plate edges more if necessary.

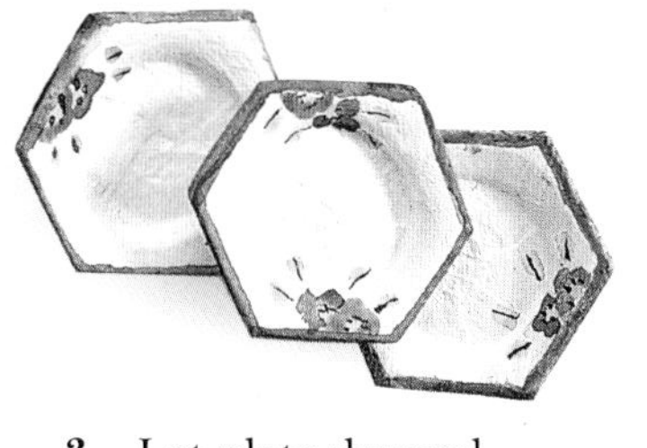

3 ~ Let plate dry and neaten edges with sandpaper before painting.

WORKING WITH WOOD

When choosing wood, the most important thing is that it be free of knots and cracks. Sheets of 2 mm ($^1/_{16}$ in) obeche (basswood) strip and single-ply plywood are the recommended craft woods. They are lightweight, easy to cut, and take well to staining. Spruce and pine are harder to work with. A great many other wood products come in handy for doll's house decorating including dowel, squared strip, decorative mouldings, and cocktail sticks. Always sand wood pieces before assembling so you have a nice, smooth finish, and stain before glueing (see right). Use fine sandpaper.

Masking tape is used to roughly assemble pieces

Glue should be all-purpose, strong, clear plastic adhesive

Rulers are necessary to mark measurements. A metal ruler can be used to cut against for a straight edge; a plastic ruler can be used to mark directly onto wood

Cutting tools include a craft knife or scalpel; a scissors can sometimes be used

Obeche (basswood) comes in various thicknesses and widths; the widest is 75 mm (3 in). I've used 2mm ($^1/_{16}$ in) thick strip as my basic construction wood throughout the book

Squared strip comes in various widths and is used for legs, rails, and toy construction

Essential Woodworking Tools

A mini craft saw and mitre box make doll's house carpentry simple. A mitre box is essential for cutting squared corners and for getting a clean straight edge. It has indentations that match the standard craft wood widths so that your wood is held firmly. A lip at the front can be positioned at the edge of the workbench in case you need to apply traction.

Single-ply plywood is thinner than obeche (basswood) but comes in larger widths. It is useful for the backs of wardrobes

Cocktail sticks are useful for legs, umbrella handles, and plate racks

Dowel comes in various thicknesses and can be used for legs, rails, broom handles, and bedposts

Sandpaper can be wound around a pencil and used to smooth curves

Mouldings can be used for decorative edgings

How to make a **Picture Frame**

1 ~ Having selected your picture, decide on the size of the frame, i.e. whether it is to fit the picture exactly or accommodate a mount.

2 ~ Measure from outer edge to get accurate lengths then cut one back piece and four sides, mitring the corners of the sides.

3 ~ Stick picture to backing then glue on frame pieces. Attach to wall using a thread or fuse wire handle or use double-sided tape.

How to make a **Kitchen Shelf**

1 ~ Transfer templates to wood and cut out. Using a piece of sandpaper wrapped around a wooden block, sand pieces down to get a nice finish and to neaten curves.

2 ~ Check for fit by roughly assembling pieces with masking tape. Stain with a proprietary product or strong tea, if desired (see below).

3 ~ When pieces are dry, apply glue to the sides and back and stick together. Then glue sides and back of shelves and slot into place. Hold unit with an elastic band until glue sets.

Staining

Water-based stains are available from most craft and DIY shops. Alway apply stain before glue, as glue will form an impenetrable barrier and prevent the stain reaching the wood underneath. Brewed tea makes a good pine or light oak finish. Both tea and proprietary stain should be applied with a brush, and several coats can be applied where a darker stain is wanted. Most stains are dry within 30 to 60 minutes. If you are adding a lace trim to resemble woodwork, this can be stained as well.

Pine or light oak is best achieved by strong tea

Dark oak or other hardwoods will require a proprietary wood stain

WORKING WITH FABRICS

Fabrics are essential to the doll's house decorator for pillows, cushions, curtains, wall hangings, tablecloths, bed linen and hangings, covering walls and floors, lining wardrobes and screens, and clothes. In addition to fabric, a wide range of trimmings and threads also comes in handy. An all-purpose, strong clear adhesive and a glue stick are useful for sticking fabric to furniture and dolls. Fabric sealer is a proprietary product sold to stop fraying; clear nail varnish can be used.

Ribbon roses are good for finishing off bolsters, pillows, and hat boxes

Ribbon is used for trimming furniture and hat boxes, wrapping around linens, and as hinges

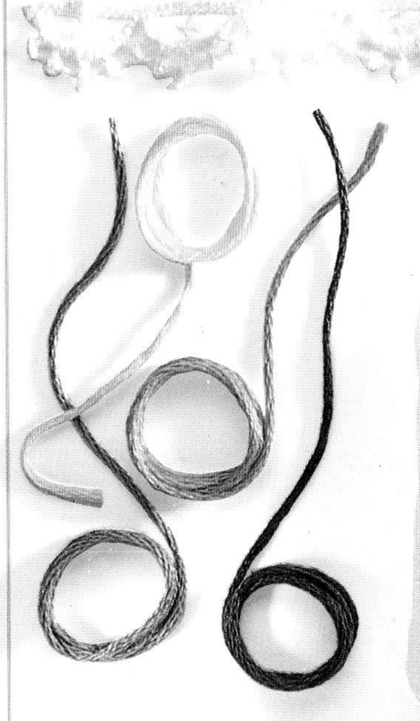

Lace fabric is used for doilies, tablecloths, curtains and trimmings; lace trim can be used as "carving" if stiffened by painting or staining

Fringe is used around the edge of furniture and for pelmets and canopies

Embroidery threads are used for dolls' hair, brush bristles, and for embroidered trim

Wadding is essential for padding furniture and dolls; stuff it with lavender for a nice aroma

Towelling is used for bath mats, toilet covers, and towels. A stretchy terrycloth is ideal

Canvas and woven fabric is used for working carpets and rugs, stool covers, samplers and cushions

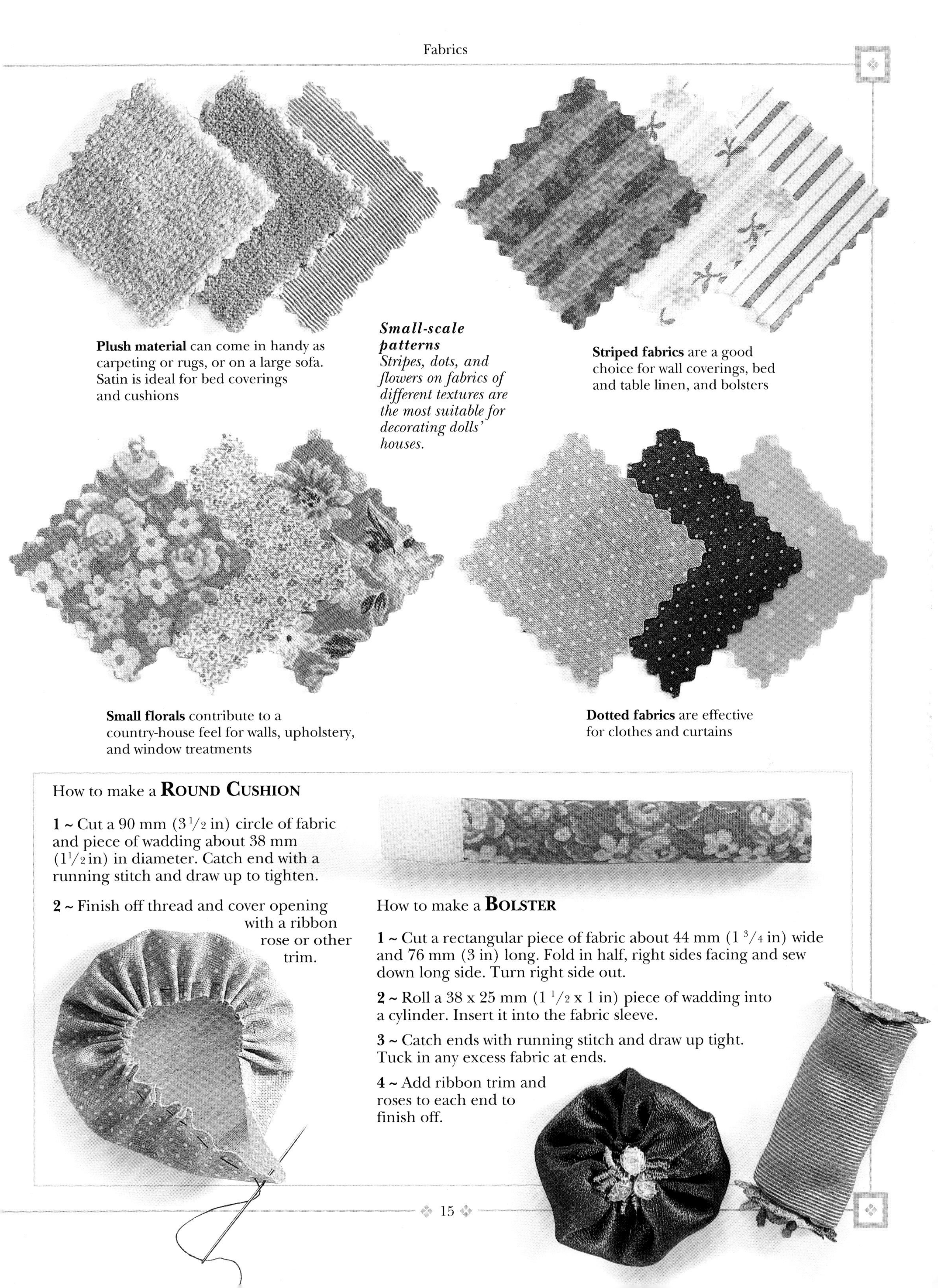

Plush material can come in handy as carpeting or rugs, or on a large sofa. Satin is ideal for bed coverings and cushions

Small-scale patterns
Stripes, dots, and flowers on fabrics of different textures are the most suitable for decorating dolls' houses.

Striped fabrics are a good choice for wall coverings, bed and table linen, and bolsters

Small florals contribute to a country-house feel for walls, upholstery, and window treatments

Dotted fabrics are effective for clothes and curtains

How to make a **Round Cushion**

1 ~ Cut a 90 mm (3 $1/2$ in) circle of fabric and piece of wadding about 38 mm (1$1/2$ in) in diameter. Catch end with a running stitch and draw up to tighten.

2 ~ Finish off thread and cover opening with a ribbon rose or other trim.

How to make a **Bolster**

1 ~ Cut a rectangular piece of fabric about 44 mm (1 $3/4$ in) wide and 76 mm (3 in) long. Fold in half, right sides facing and sew down long side. Turn right side out.

2 ~ Roll a 38 x 25 mm (1 $1/2$ x 1 in) piece of wadding into a cylinder. Insert it into the fabric sleeve.

3 ~ Catch ends with running stitch and draw up tight. Tuck in any excess fabric at ends.

4 ~ Add ribbon trim and roses to each end to finish off.

WORKING WITH PAINT

A selection of acrylic paints and a primer is all that is needed for paper, self-hardening clay and wood, but water colours can be used as well. Acrylic primer can be used on all materials as a base on which to add surface decoration. Gold and silver paints are ideal for creating metallic finishes, and a variety of felt-tips and markers can be used for creating embroidery effects on paper and fabric.

Acrylic paints and a primer are used for crockery, creating raised effects on furniture, for making doll's faces, and for strengthening furniture made of cardboard and paper. The acrylic primer dries quickly and gives a good surface to items making them take the paint better

Gold and silver paints are used for kitchen utensils, for making pails, knobs and taps, and for adding certain trims, such as on decorative boxes

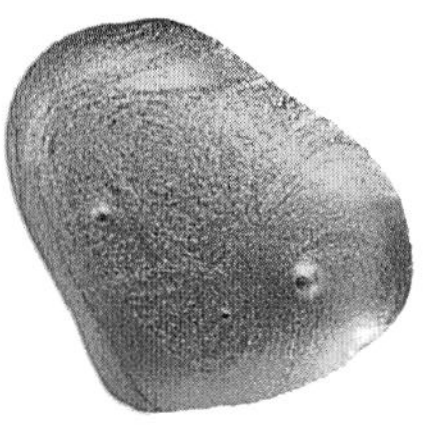

Varnish should be used on self-hardening clay and wood to give a sheen and richness of effect. This should be an acetone-based clear varnish

Water colours such as a child's paintbox set come in handy for painting paper items or pictures

Felt-tip pens and markers add colour to shower curtains and hot water bottle jackets, and are used for patchwork effects and lettering on sacks

WORKING WITH BITS AND PIECES

A variety of natural and manufactured items are ideal for using in a doll's house. A walnut shell, for example, makes a fine baby's bed and small-scale foods can be substituted for the real thing. With a little imagination, you'll soon see an alternative use for practically every little object that you come across.

Beads of all types are useful. Little coloured beads are ideal for knobs, pulls, and jewels while larger wooden beads are used as furniture feet. Crystal beads can be used as inkwells, and topped with smaller beads. Venetian or decorative beads can be used as vases or containers. Hollow beads can be used as goblets or dishes

Sequins can be used when creating bouquets and other flower arrangements

Pearls come in different sizes. Small ones can be dotted onto furniture and bedcovers, or used as jewellery, or drawer knobs

Felt-tip pen tops can be cut to size to form blender jars and milkshake glasses in stands of modelling medium

Buttons can be used as picture frames and as clock faces

Plastic containers can be shaped to use as inset glass doors on washing machines and dryers, or as cheese domes

Jewellery findings, which include small rings, nose studs, chains, and oval holders can be used for jewellery, picture frames, and hanging chains

Paper clips can be used as pendulums or trolley feet

Sponges both real and manufactured can be used as their full-grown cousins

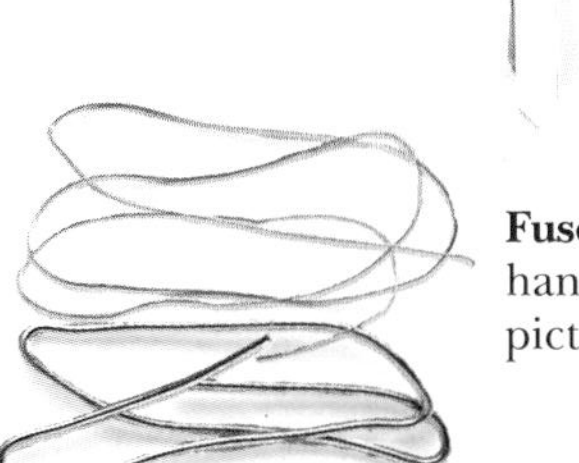

Fuse wire is useful for pail handles and for hanging pictures

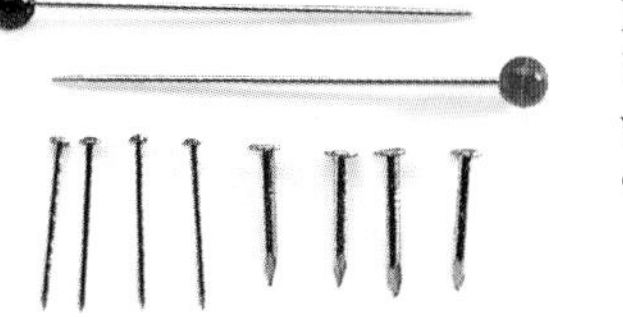

Pins and nails – gold-headed, beaded or pearlized and of varying sizes – can be used as drawer and door knobs

Dried beans and seeds can be painted and used for knobs; other "real" food can be used to stock kitchen canisters

Feathers can be used in dusters and on dolls' hats

THE VICTORIAN

KITCHEN

This fully equipped downstairs kitchen is the scene of ceaseless activity. Cook is always in evidence, and the housemaids bustle in and out with tea trays and cleaning supplies. Furnishings are utilitarian with few creature comforts for the staff. The old cast-iron stove, with its ever-burning fire, requires constant feeding, and the range of cast-iron pots hints at the number of hungry mouths to feed.

The big dresser to the left houses a variety of staple items in its cupboards while the shelves hold several storage canisters. Nearby, jams and preserves are stored on a wall-hung unit.

Next to the range, a small wooden table, useful for holding cooking utensils, sits beneath a drying rack. The large butler's sink to the right is supported on pillars of "brick" and has a "Delft tile" splashback to match that of the range. Only cold water comes out of the tap; hot water is heated in the kettle.

The large central pine table is where most of the food is prepared. It has to be big enough for rolling out pastry and sorting the produce from the kitchen garden or greengrocer's. When it is below stairs' tea time, the table is set with crockery and the high-backed chairs are drawn up close.

The big Welsh dresser by the window is where the china is kept. When not in use, the cutlery is stored in its commodious drawers.

Tile splashback, here and on sink, is specially printed doll's house paper

Organically grown produce
Untouched by harmful fertilizers and sprays, the weekly produce delivery, made from modelling medium, has to be sorted and stored.

Drying rack for dishes
has cocktail stick slotted shelves that fit into wood strip back and sides

Welsh dresser
has embroidered ribbon trim added to its top for a sprightly decorative finish

Housemaid's box
of wood strip has black modelling medium "wrought iron" handle and brackets

Towel rack
is made from squared strip pieces taped together

Floor rug
has fringe made by removing several woof threads from its woven fabric

Wallcovering and floor
– the one being a flower-sprigged fabric, the other brick paper sheeting – approximate to Victorian originals

THE VICTORIAN KITCHEN CATALOGUE

Dinner service
All manner of gaily coloured plates, platters, cups, saucers, tureens, bowls, sauceboats, and other eating and serving crockery can be created from self-hardening clay shaped and then painted. See page 11 for how-to instructions.

Farm-fresh vegetables
Not a trace of pests or weather damage on a range of produce modelled to please. No doll-house child would dare leave over his or her vegetables. See page 11 for tips.

The kitchen clock
A coin-sized circle of modelling medium has a smaller white face painted on it; numbers and hands are picked out in black.

Baskets, bags, and boxes
The essential containers for a range of stock ingredients are created out of paper, fabric, and modelling medium. The potatoes, mushrooms, apples, and eggs are of modelling medium, too.

Delicious edibles
The groaning board will be limited only by your imagination and skill in modelling foodstuffs for every meal; see page 28 for more.

Calendar
Frozen in time or kept up to date, an old-fashioned farmhouse calendar of ply-wood and paper is easy to read.

Spice storage
Tiny pieces of wood are all that's needed to make the drawers to house your spice selection and a box to keep salt running free.

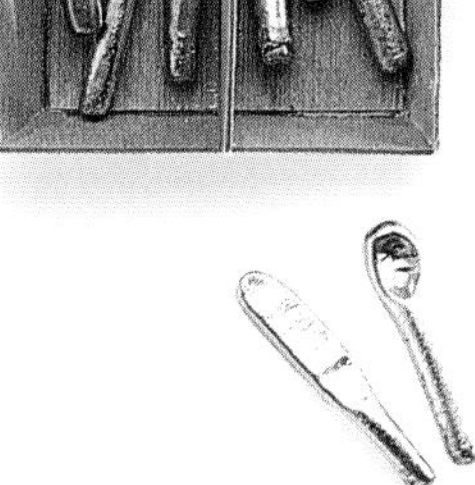

Jugs and bowls
Pitchers for pouring cream, milk, and juice, and bowls to house fresh-picked strawberries, ice creams, and puddings are shaped out of self-hardening clay and painted in delicate patterns. See page 11 for how-to instructions.

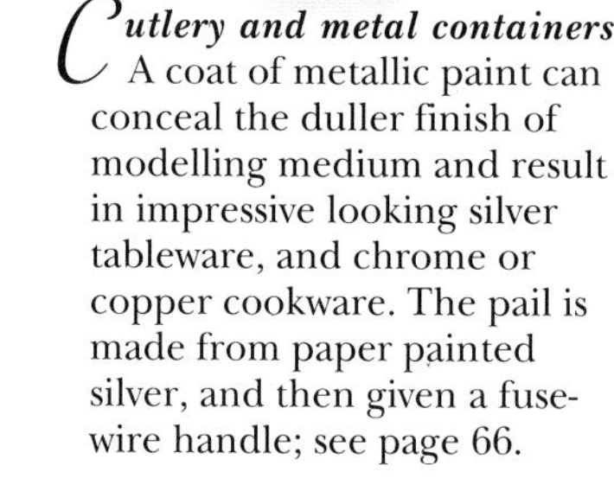

Cutlery and metal containers
A coat of metallic paint can conceal the duller finish of modelling medium and result in impressive looking silver tableware, and chrome or copper cookware. The pail is made from paper painted silver, and then given a fuse-wire handle; see page 66.

Pots and pans
Sturdy cookware designed to withstand the heat of the old-fashioned range can be made in a variety of styles from modelling medium; the heat-driven irons are similarly created.

Home-made preserves
Rows of gingham-covered jars housing last summer's bounty can stock larder shelves or be put out on display. Make them out of modelling medium in the appropriate colours to reflect the contents.

Floor-cleaning materials
Mops, brooms, brushes, dustpans, and other assorted sweeping gear can be fashioned out of dowel or cocktail sticks and given embroidery thread or modelling medium bristles.

Baking utensils
A rolling pin and an assortment of mixing spoons are modelled to look like wood. The mortar and pestle are well served by the original substance.

Cleaning box
The wood strip and modelling medium box contains brushes, with embroidery thread bristles, shoe polish of modelling medium, a fabric cleaning rag, and a real feather duster.

THE VICTORIAN KITCHEN FURNITURE

KITCHEN DRESSER

Ideal for displaying crockery or holding ample supplies, two dressers can be created from the templates on page 68. The Welsh dresser shown here and described on page 69 uses all the templates except for the base and drawer panel. For an open-shelved one, use the drawer panel front, add an extra shelf, and finish with the base piece.

LARGE RECTANGULAR TABLE

Similar in construction to the small rectangular table, see right, this has a 75 x 125 mm (3 x 5 in) wood strip top.

Four 12 mm (1/2 in) wide side pieces of wood strip – two of 65 mm (2 9/16 in), and two of 115 mm (4 9/16 in) – should be glued together to make the support frame for the top.

Four legs 65 mm (2 9/16 in) long should be cut from squared strip and glued one into each corner. Two 55 mm (2 1/8 in) squared strip pieces are used for cross braces to hold shelf.

A 40 x 110 mm (1 9/16 x 4 5/16 in) piece of single-ply plywood forms a lower shelf and is glued to the cross braces.

Two wood drawer fronts, 32 x 6 mm (1 1/4 x 1/4 in), have modelling medium knobs glued on.

"Pine" finish comes from staining with tea

To finish off the curves, wrap a piece of sandpaper around a pencil and use to sand away any excess wood

Decorative ribbon trim is glued to a thin strip of wood then attached to the dresser

Legs are of 6 mm (1/4 in) squared strip

Top and frame are made of wood strip

Paper "tile" easy-to-clean surface

Sink Unit

This sturdy butler's sink of self-hardening clay painted with white acrylic stands on two massive wooden supports – 45 mm deep x 16 mm wide x 52 mm high ($1^3/_4$ x $^5/_8$ x 2 in) – covered in brick paper.

The splashback is a piece of cardboard, 75 x 115 mm (3 x $4^1/_2$ in), painted white. It is decorated with tile-printed paper, and supports a tap of grey modelling medium.

Integral shelf to store pots and pans

Hinges cut from gold stars

Kitchen Stove

Essential for hot water and heat, this solid fuel-burning range of cardboard painted with black acrylic, has its templates on pages 78-79.

Fire of red, orange, yellow, and black tissue paper

Knobs are split peas painted gold

Small Rectangular Table

One or more of these "pine" tables with integral drawer are very handy in a kitchen for storing utensils or holding plates of food. Full making-up instructions and templates are on page 69.

High-Backed Chair

Any number of these simple "pine" kitchen chairs can be created using the templates and written instructions for the wooden chair on page 80. They also look nice with decorative seat cushions (see page 28).

THE MODERN KITCHEN

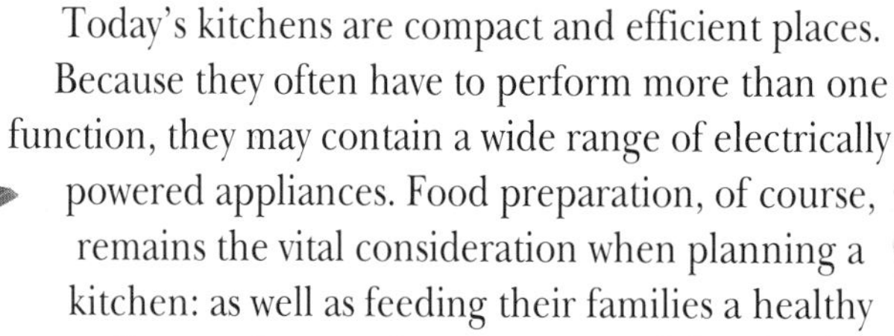

Today's kitchens are compact and efficient places. Because they often have to perform more than one function, they may contain a wide range of electrically powered appliances. Food preparation, of course, remains the vital consideration when planning a kitchen: as well as feeding their families a healthy diet, modern cooks are concerned that food preparation be quick and easy, so today's kitchens come equipped with many labour-saving devices.

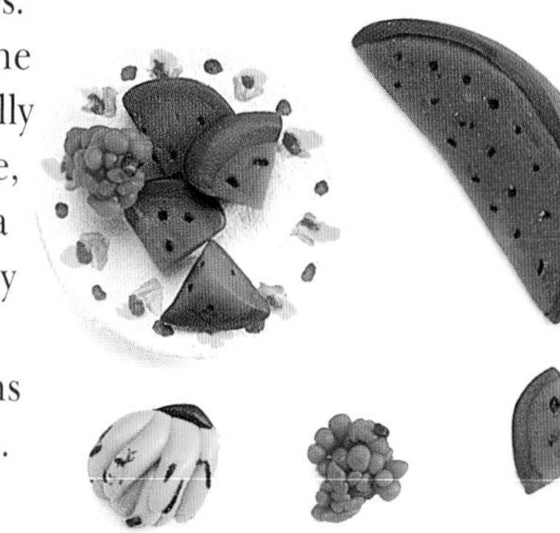

Fresh fruit
Watermelon slices, grapes, and bananas of modelling medium are a colourful and healthful addition in any kitchen. They make an ideal snack or a delicious dessert.

Vegetable medley
Today's generation enjoys peppers, broccoli, tomatoes, cabbage, mushrooms, asparagus, and cucumbers in salads, and new potatoes simply boiled. The vegetables are freshly modelled. The mushroom box is paper, the basket modelling medium, and the potato dirt, cocoa.

Cake tins
Gaily decorated paper containers hold tea-time snacks of biscuits and an iced chocolate cake. The biscuits and cake, including the glacé cherries, are all created from modelling medium.

Everyday dishes
An assortment of plates and mugs are created from self-hardening clay and are decorated with a sprightly flower motif. They are dishwasher safe.

Kitchen knives
Silver painted paper blades are set into modelling medium handles. They are stored on a silver paper-and-wood rack.

Electrical appliances
The tea kettle and blender base are modelled while the microwave is cardboard.

Pin board and holder
Ideal for displaying shopping lists and reminders, the pin board is constructed of paper and wood. Paper towels are stored on a wall-mounted holder.

Spice rack
A variety of dried herbs and spices are stored in jars of modelling medium set on a wall-hung wooden unit. The two storage drawers have gold headed pin pulls.

Glass canisters
The jars are made from plastic tubes, used to hold glitter, and the tops are of modelling medium. They store millet "puffed rice", wholemeal spaghetti, flour, and sesame seed "dried beans".

Iron and board
The wooden board with fabric and silver tape trim stands on painted wire legs. The steam iron is made of modelling medium.

Bread board
A wooden circle serves as cutting board for modelled loaves. The French bread, fresh from the baker, stands in a paper bag.

The Efficiency Kitchen

Where space is at a premium, furnishings need to maximize the available space. A stacking cardboard washer and dryer have plastic-lid windows set in a silver painted and tape trim surround. These halve the amount of floor space normally required. The wooden stool and paper-and-wire storage unit can be stored under the wood, bead, and dowel worktop.

THE COLONIAL KITCHEN

Popular with period decorators, American colonial interiors have a particular rustic charm. Lacking any modern comforts and conveniences, inhabitants of dolls' houses of the time will have to make do with mainly plain and unadorned kitchen equipment and accessories. In addition to their often rough and ready designs, they are notable for their being constructed of widely available materials – wood, straw, and clay.

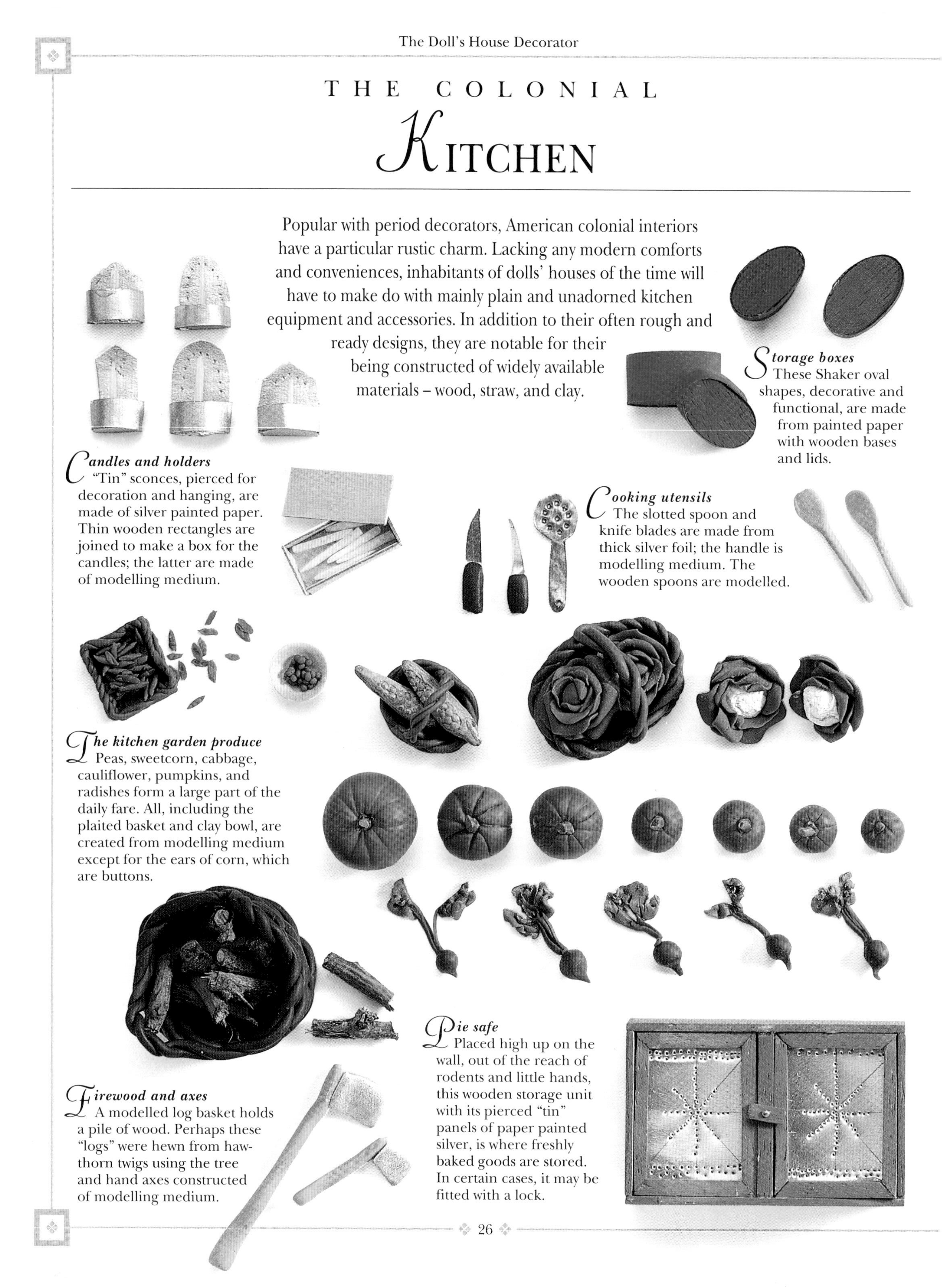

Storage boxes
These Shaker oval shapes, decorative and functional, are made from painted paper with wooden bases and lids.

Candles and holders
"Tin" sconces, pierced for decoration and hanging, are made of silver painted paper. Thin wooden rectangles are joined to make a box for the candles; the latter are made of modelling medium.

Cooking utensils
The slotted spoon and knife blades are made from thick silver foil; the handle is modelling medium. The wooden spoons are modelled.

The kitchen garden produce
Peas, sweetcorn, cabbage, cauliflower, pumpkins, and radishes form a large part of the daily fare. All, including the plaited basket and clay bowl, are created from modelling medium except for the ears of corn, which are buttons.

Pie safe
Placed high up on the wall, out of the reach of rodents and little hands, this wooden storage unit with its pierced "tin" panels of paper painted silver, is where freshly baked goods are stored. In certain cases, it may be fitted with a lock.

Firewood and axes
A modelled log basket holds a pile of wood. Perhaps these "logs" were hewn from hawthorn twigs using the tree and hand axes constructed of modelling medium.

Pioneering Pastimes

The hub of colonial life is the kitchen and there, a doll's house denizen will find lots to do. The fire needs feeding for the cooking pot or hot water, clothes need washing, produce from the garden needs sorting and preparing and, when there is a spare moment, there's always the mending to pick up and see to.

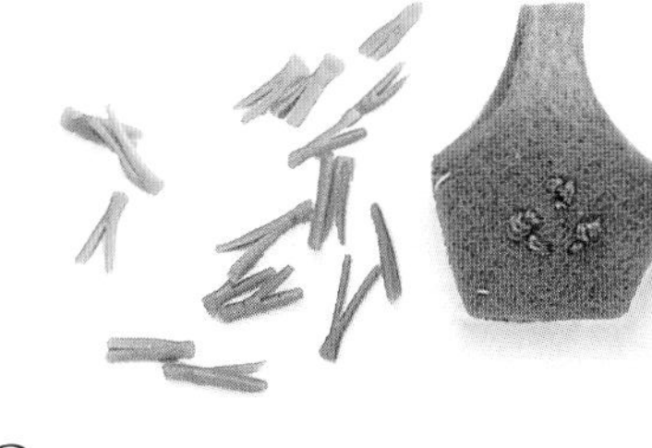

Clothes washing paraphenalia
The wash tub of painted paper and the clothes scrubber – painted paper with wooden sides – are familiar kitchen items as the open fire provided the hot water needed for cleaning clothes. The modelled clothes pins in their felt holder would have hung on a nearby wall until needed.

Hat rack
Brass headed pins on two rectangular wooden strips make a simple and effective storage place.
The pouches, used for holding powder and bullets, were made of leather scraps, while the gardening hat was created from plaited straw and has a beaded trim.

Patchwork
Miniature fabric squares are glued to a backing to suggest the floor coverings created from worn-out clothes. The sewing threads and pin cushion are of modelling medium, the box is wood.

Canisters and jugs
The "stoneware" canisters, made of modelling medium, are useful for keeping dry goods, such as sugar and flour, free from pests while the jugs store cider, maple syrup, and molasses.

FOOD FROM THE KITCHEN

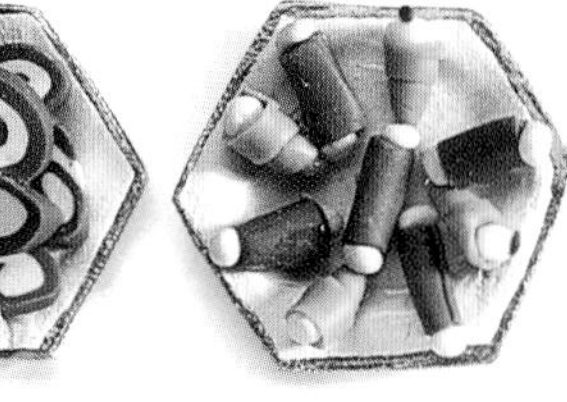

Any doll's house cook worth her salt must be able to provide three square meals a day, and a host of party and special occasion dishes. Luckily, all he or she needs is modelling material in a variety of colours, some self-hardening clay or buttons for the plates, and proper photographic reference. Then every culinary occasion – from Sunday brunch through to a tea party, picnic, or even Christmas dinner – can be celebrated in style.

Glorious Cakes
Chocolate cupcakes, each topped with a cherry or candy, accompany a lemon layer cake covered with marzipan icing. These, plus the Black Forest gâteau, are sure to suit every doll's sweet tooth. The plates are made similar to those on page 11, and painted white with a gold trim.

Perfect Pastries
Chocolate cream pie in a chocolate pastry crust, slices of Swiss roll, and cream filled chocolate and pastry rolls, are ideal tea-time treats. For the Swiss roll effect, top a rectangular layer of brown "cake" with one of white and roll up both together.

Middle Eastern Specialties
Pita breads filled with salad and meat or cheese are on offer alongside lamb kebabs threaded onto pins.

All-American Fare
Hamburgers in buns with chips and a salad garnish are standard snack-time orders. Serve with plenty of modelled tomato ketchup and salt and pepper.

A Christmas Feast
The traditional golden roasted turkey, mince pies, and plum pudding are joined by a selection of fresh vegetables including carrots, peas, and potatoes, with a fresh berry cocktail to follow.

The Festive Table
Dressed in a seasonal cloth with bows and golden trim, the best bead goblets and "china" plates are complemented by the wreathed candle centrepiece. Paper crackers are there for the pulling.

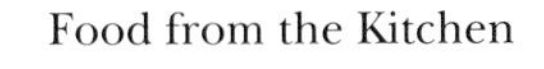

Meals for all Occasions
Party planning was never easier for the doll's house entertainer. Modelling medium is ideal for creating a vast number of special dishes suitable for all types of meals. Set food on a piece of the appropriate fabric, accompany with matching napkins or paper decorations, serve on a few painted self-hardening clay plates, and you can create the culinary ambiance of your choice.

Different coloured party streamers add to the fun

"Plates" are white plastic buttons in dinner and serving plate sizes

A small amount of fabric is all that is required to make a cloth and napkin set

A Child's Party
Make it a really special occasion by serving up food certain to please the younger set – hot dogs, chunks of cheese, ice cream cones and sundaes, iced biscuits, jelly, and a rose decorated pink-frosted cake.

Sunday Brunch
Platefuls of eggs, bacon, and sausage are salmonella- and cholesterol-free. Enjoy them with mushrooms and grilled tomatoes. Select toast or the breakfast roll of your choice and spread with butter or strawberry jam.

High Tea
This substantial early evening meal, first indulged in over a century ago, is made up primarily of cold meats, savoury pies, and sandwiches. A more contemporary addition is the selection of imported cheeses.

Pies and terrines can be recreated with a variety of fillings and in all the traditional shapes

Red-topped Edam and ripe Brie accompany two foil-wrapped cheeses

THE VICTORIAN

Master Bedroom

Off limits to all but the littlest one, the master bedroom's decoration owes much to Mama's taste. She regards it as her refuge from the cares of running a large house. Although she has little time for breakfast in bed now that baby has arrived, today is a special day. Along with morning tea in her special china set, a beautiful bouquet, to mark her wedding anniversary, arrived on the breakfast tray.

Pride of place in the room is held by the grand four-poster, one item of the bedroom suite that formed part of her dowry. The moiré satin bed hangings, bolster, and coverlet were imported from France, created to her specifications. The fabric-covered dressing table with lace trim and the pearl-buttoned boudoir chair complete the set. Set on top of the dressing table is Mama's jewellery casket, grooming set, and some jars of face cream. Displayed on the small table next to the bed and on the walls are a number of family photographs.

Mama also brought some other good furniture pieces with her on her marriage. These include the antique sewing basket, of which she makes much use – with the children and household furnishings to see to – and the mahogany chest of drawers.

Papa's silk waistcoat, only worn on special days, is displayed on the wooden valet; he will wear it today to please Mama.

Wild flower print of dried forget-me-nots complements delicate floral wallpaper

Lace-skirted cradle of eggshells with fabric trim makes a snug bed for baby

Four-poster bed of cardboard and wooden dowel has elaborate moiré satin bed hangings

Family photographs are miniature illustrations set in jewellery finding frames

Anniversary bouquet *contains beads set on sequins held by embroidery thread*

Modesty screen of wooden panels has transfer decoration

Parasols are fabric scraps glued to cocktail sticks and topped with beads

Mama's little luxuries
A present of a Paris hat, in its beautiful beribboned box, and lace parasol brings a twinkle to her eyes.

THE VICTORIAN MASTER BEDROOM CATALOGUE

Dressing table accessories
Modelling medium is used for the lavender wand drawer fresheners, brushes, and pin cushion base.

Table-top mirror
Silvered plastic "mirror" is glued to a wooden frame. Two drawers with bead pulls store delicate fabric hankies. The stud boxes are buttons.

Tea service
Delicate milk glass tea set with matching cups and saucers is arranged on cloth-covered wooden tray. The china and lemon cake slices are all of modelling medium.

Hat boxes
Floral patterned fabric is glued to circular cardboard boxes decorated with ribbon and lace trim and used for protecting special-occasion hats. Placed on top of a wardrobe they are pretty and practical storage items. See page 9 for how-to.

Hats and bonnets
Scraps of satin, wool, and felt fabrics are augmented by feathers and ribbon trims to produce a range of headwear suitable for most occasions.

Family jewels
A casket (and key) of silver wedding-cake trim stores jewellery constructed of wire, beads, and brilliants.

Parasols
Lengths of satin fabric with ribbon and lace trim are furled around painted cocktail sticks with bead ends.

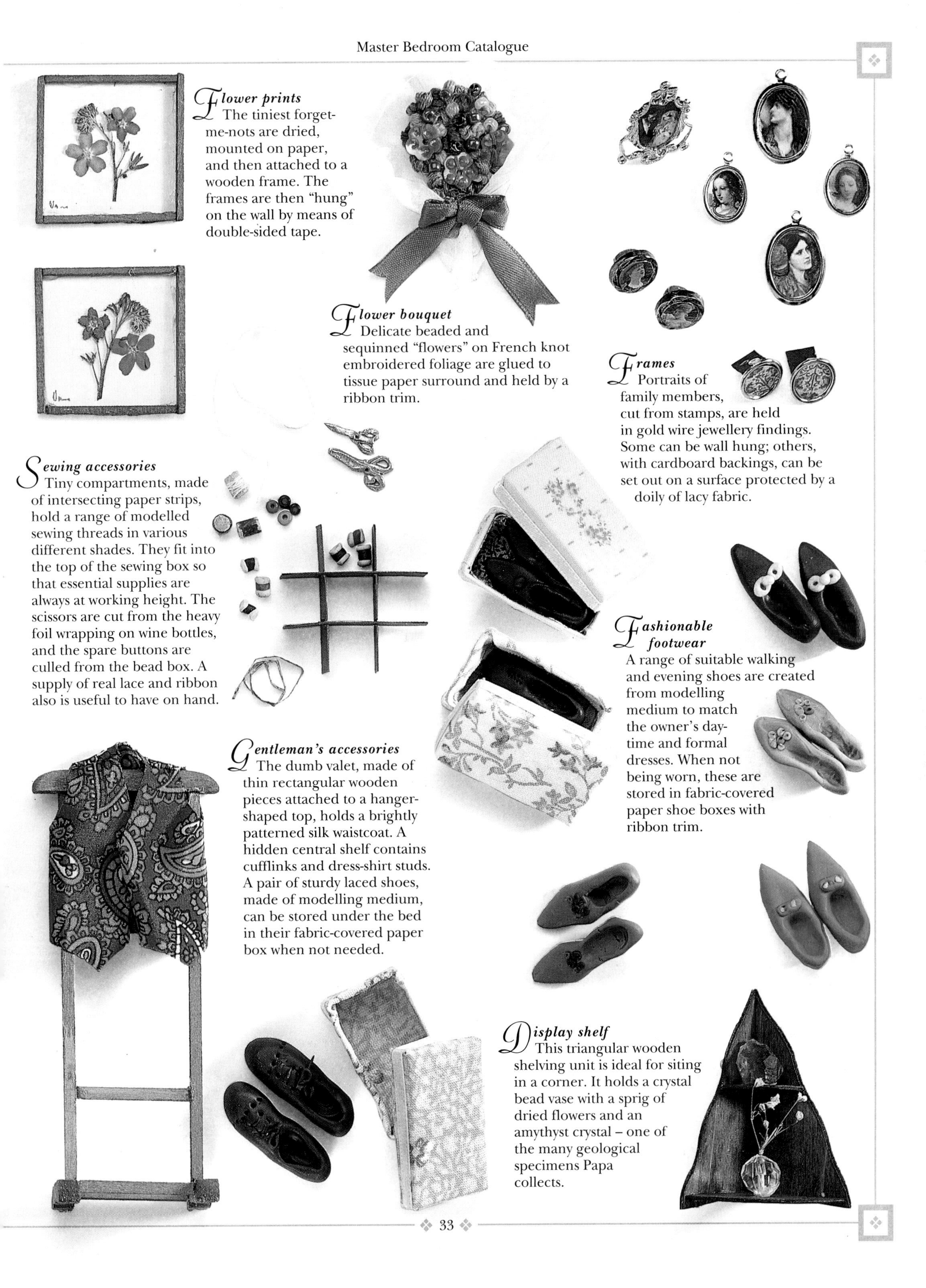

Flower prints
The tiniest forget-me-nots are dried, mounted on paper, and then attached to a wooden frame. The frames are then "hung" on the wall by means of double-sided tape.

Flower bouquet
Delicate beaded and sequinned "flowers" on French knot embroidered foliage are glued to tissue paper surround and held by a ribbon trim.

Frames
Portraits of family members, cut from stamps, are held in gold wire jewellery findings. Some can be wall hung; others, with cardboard backings, can be set out on a surface protected by a doily of lacy fabric.

Sewing accessories
Tiny compartments, made of intersecting paper strips, hold a range of modelled sewing threads in various different shades. They fit into the top of the sewing box so that essential supplies are always at working height. The scissors are cut from the heavy foil wrapping on wine bottles, and the spare buttons are culled from the bead box. A supply of real lace and ribbon also is useful to have on hand.

Fashionable footwear
A range of suitable walking and evening shoes are created from modelling medium to match the owner's day-time and formal dresses. When not being worn, these are stored in fabric-covered paper shoe boxes with ribbon trim.

Gentleman's accessories
The dumb valet, made of thin rectangular wooden pieces attached to a hanger-shaped top, holds a brightly patterned silk waistcoat. A hidden central shelf contains cufflinks and dress-shirt studs. A pair of sturdy laced shoes, made of modelling medium, can be stored under the bed in their fabric-covered paper box when not needed.

Display shelf
This triangular wooden shelving unit is ideal for siting in a corner. It holds a crystal bead vase with a sprig of dried flowers and an amythyst crystal – one of the many geological specimens Papa collects.

THE VICTORIAN MASTER BEDROOM FURNITURE

4-Poster Bed

Deserving of pride of place in any bedroom, this king-sized bed is covered in a substantial moiré fabric, which is used for the quilted bed cover, canopy, and valance. Hidden from view is a padded mattress covered with handkerchief fabric sheets and a top blanket of embroidered felt. For templates and making-up instructions, see page 76.

Lacy fabric is glued to cradle hood

Eggshell halves make the ideal cradle for youngest family member

Canopy with embroidered flower trim

Two layered skirt has a simple underskirt topped with lacy covering

Infant Cradle

The body of the cradle is an eggshell half supported within a circular card base 5 cm (2 in) high. The cradle hood is another eggshell half placed perpendicular to the body. Lace fabric is glued to the hood. A piece of plain white fabric, topped with a layer of lace, is attached around the perimeter of the body to form a generous skirt.

Matching bed cover has diamond-shaped quilting and is dotted with seed pearls

Mahogany finish is produced by wood stain

Transfer motif is rubbed down on or glued to each frame

Modesty Screen

Made of wood strip pieces stained a darker shade and joined with masking tape, see page 69 for templates and instructions, this has a "gold leaf" rub-down decorative trim.

Wedding cake trim is used to decorate casket

Chest of Drawers

The pearl-knobbed deep drawers of this wooden chest hold substantial amounts of garments. Full making-up instructions and templates are on page 75.

Dressing Table

Along with its matching chair, this is part of a furniture suite that includes the 4-poster bed. Full making-up instructions and templates are found on page 66.

Cushion is filled with sand to plump it up

Boudoir Chair

The base is a 4 cm ($1^1/_2$ in) card cube and the back is made from two 9 x 4 cm ($3^1/_2$ x $1^9/_{16}$ in) card rectangles with angled tops. First the cube base is covered in the moiré fabric. Then the front-facing back piece is covered with wadding and topped with fabric, and the second fabric-covered piece is glued to it, back to back. This gives a neat effect.

The back is then glued to one side of the cube. For the seat's trim apply cut-out lace and decorative ribbon.

Attach seed pearls to the chair back. Make a cushion from matching fabric, and fill with sand to weight it.

Carved trim is lace that is stained and glued in place

Sewing Box

The separate compartments are ideal for holding a collection of sewing implements, trimmings, and threads at table-top height. For templates and making-up instructions, see page 67.

THE VICTORIAN

Girl's Bedroom

A girl's bedroom affords wonderful opportunities for making furnishings and accessories with a truly feminine feel. What young lady, no matter the era, could resist a dreamy half-tester bed dressed with pristine linen and a matching coverlet, or a wardrobe filled with cotton shifts and frilly dresses.

The pink-painted furniture harkens back to an earlier time but is just as pleasing to the contemporary child; this is a room where childhood dreams are encouraged and inspired. A bedside table can be used to hold ornaments or take a period pitcher and bowl, while the linen-topped fabric covered table is an attractive surface when she wants to draw or write. The tiny ribbon-trimmed stool and flouncy fabric chair are ideal for sitting or for putting things on.

The room is filled with items to keep a small one amused and there is a plethora of pretty, ribbon bedecked hatboxes to store toys and accessories.

A combination of floral patterns on the furniture and walls gives an English country-house feel to the room. Delightful touches such as the rose tie-backs on the curtains and embroidered flowers on the linens help to accentuate the floral theme. The commercially made wall lights are attuned to the period; everything else is hand-made, from the simply stitched sampler to the needlepointed rug.

Hatboxes, trimmed in ribbon and lace, are easy to construct from card; see instructions page 9

Half-tester bed, with its matching valance and quilted coverlet, has embroidered linens of fine cotton. Making-up instructions are on page 41

Embroidered sampler, created from fine woven fabric and silk thread, is held in a mitred frame

Accessories *are fashioned from fabric and modelling medium*

Doll's house comes with all fixtures and furnishings. Templates and instructions are on page 73

Dolly has painted bead face and modelling medium body. Her hair is embroidery thread

Toybox treasures
The teddy of self-hardening clay is a favourite toy as is the skipping rope (seen above) made from crochet thread and beads, the pull-along lamb, and scrap book.

Floor carpet is a piece of heavy duty plush fabric cut to size

THE VICTORIAN GIRL'S ROOM CATALOGUE

Sampler
A small rectangle of woven fabric is covered in letters picked out in fine silk diagonal threads. It is set within a mitred frame; for framing hints, see page 13.

Nursery animals
No self-respecting doll's house child would be without one or two of these painted clay bears. The lamb pull-toy is created from black pipe cleaners covered with bits of fleece.

A trio of dollies
Bead heads, covered in embroidery thread and set on wire bodies padded with masking tape, are covered by scraps of fabric glued to fit.

Slippers, shoes, and hangers
Embroidered terry towelling scuffs sit next to modelling medium shoes with bead trim. The fuse-wire hangers are covered in fabric scraps.

Hats
Bits of felt and ribbon are finished off with rose ribbons.

Scraps
Decorative scraps and illustrations cut from magazines can be stored in a ribbon-topped box until there is time to stick them down in paper books.

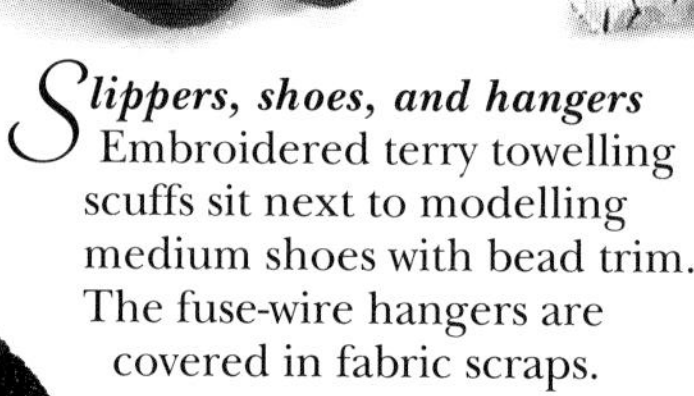

Ornamental mirror
Foil stuck to a plastic backing has a card support. Blobs of acrylic paint form the raised decorative edge.

Travelling hat boxes
These fabric-covered card containers with lace and ribbon trim come complete with embroidery thread handles for carrying. Tips on their construction can be found on page 9.

A Modern Teenager

A relatively recent "invention", the teenager must be left to her own devices when decorating. It is essential, though, to provide sufficient storage for the musical equipment, clothing accessories, and sports paraphenalia that she accumulates to overflowing.

Hot wheels
White leather red-wheeled roller skates with matching satchel for accessories are made from modelling medium.

Telephone
Modelling medium phone with painted dial has plastic spiral cord.

Art materials
Paint set and crayon pencils in decorated cases are all made from modelling medium.

Musical gear
A selection of cassette players is essential unless one wants to get out of step with the music. All are modelled.

Sweet Sixteen

Today's teenager, when home, is rarely found without her earphones or telephone! Her life is one social whirl and with all the necessary gear in tow, she is free to try her hand at a whole range of activities.

Shoulderbag
Roomy enough to hold all a girl's make-up and money, this modelled "leather" handbag has "brass" jewellery finding clasp and buckles.

Outdoor accessories
Modelling medium is ideal for creating waterproof accessories such as the pairs of rubber sandals, the drawstring beach bag, the high-factor sun lotions, and the polarized sun glasses.

THE VICTORIAN
GIRL'S ROOM FURNITURE

Interior is lined with floral fabric

WARDROBE

This fabric-lined storage unit has ample hanging and shelf space to hold all a girl's clothing. The decoration is coordinated between the external trim and the floral fabric inside. Full making-up instructions and templates are on page 74.

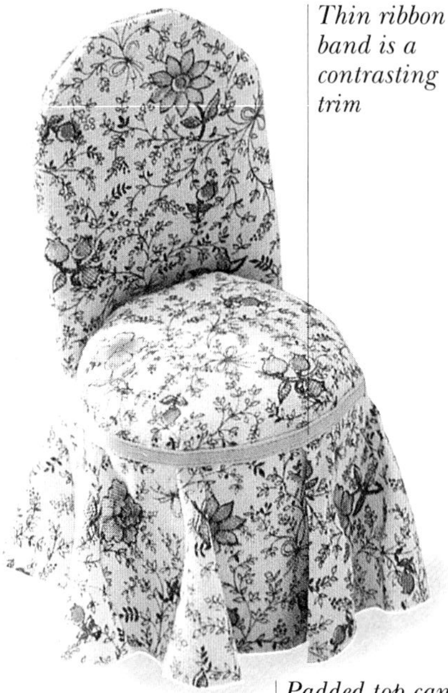

Thin ribbon band is a contrasting trim

SKIRTED CHAIR

This dressing table chair has a feminine feel with its flounced floral patterned covering. Find templates and instructions on page 73.

Knobs are made by applying acrylic paint thickly

Hinges are lengths of thin ribbon

Padded top can be used for additional seating

Fabric matches that of dressing table chair

TOYBOX

Essentially a box within a box, this commodious container can accommodate a large number of books, games, and toys. The outer cardboard rectangular box 8 x 4 x 4 cm ($3\,^1/_8$ x $1\,^9/_{16}$ x $1\,^9/_{16}$) is covered in a floral fabric.

A smaller box, 2.5 cm (1 in) high, covered in a coordinating fabric, is glued inside to the bottom and sides.

The box has a cardboard lid, topped with wadding and covered with fabric. This is finished off on the underside by a smaller rectangle covered in the coordinating fabric. The lid is attached to the box by transparent tape and thin ribbon "hinges".

Washstand

Pink-painted washstand has decorative curved detailing on its back and front. Useful for storing a girl's bits and pieces, instructions and templates are on page 72.

Pillows are embroidered with floral motif

Single-sized bed is made of cardboard and has fabric bedding

Half-Tester Bed

A close relative of the 4-poster found in the master bedroom, this dreamy girl's bed can be made by adapting the templates and instructions found on pages 76-78. A cardboard base should be formed that is 78mm (3 in) wide. A valance is created similarly to its larger relative, then neatened by a fabric-covered top piece.

The headboard of 85 x 155 mm ($3^{5}/_{16}$ x $6^{1}/_{8}$ in) cardboard is attached to the back; two fabric-covered sides, 45 x 155 mm ($1^{3}/_{4}$ x $6^{1}/_{8}$ in), and a fabric-covered top, 85 x 43mm ($3^{5}/_{16}$ x $1^{11}/_{16}$ in), are joined to it.

The half-tester top is a slightly larger rectangle, approximately 90 x 45 x 12 mm ($3^{1}/_{8}$ x $1^{3}/_{4}$ x $^{1}/_{2}$ in). This is covered in fabric and has a ruffle, trimmed with lace, glued to its under side. Two lace-trimmed curtains also are added before the tester is glued firmly to the top of the headboard. Ribbon rose tie-backs and a quilted coverlet complete the bed clothes. The pillowcases are embroidered with rose buds.

Lace-trimmed curtains are glued to back

Open-weave fabric can be embroidered

Circular Table

Identical to the sitting room table but covered in a calico skirt with woven top, the instructions and templates are on page 72.

A Victorian Boy

Less sophisticated than his modern-day counterpart, the 19th century boy is surrounded by a selection of leather-bound books, sports equipment, and sturdy toys and playthings that provide his amusement. He depends on his teddy bear for comfort.

Paper kites
Made like their bigger brothers from wood strips and paper but with thread twine, these can sail across a boy's room as well as the sky.

Drum and sticks
When he wants to sound off, our boy uses paper drum with plastic sticks cut from a comb.

School books
Bound in modelling medium "leather", these are for reading, 'riting and 'rithmatic.

Bat, ball, and box
Wood was used for the bat and box; the ball and Jack were modelled.

Boat scenes
Wood scrap frames enclose two miniature sailboats made of red-painted wood, with painted paper sails and pennants.

Slatted bed
This single bed has a head- and footboard of wood strip and legs of 6 mm (1/4 in) squared strip. The frame is squared strip with wood slats. All are stained. The bedding consists of a wadding mattress covered with fine cotton sheets and woven fabric throw. The pipe-cleaner teddy is often found sleeping there.

Tug and sail boat
The small wooden tug for bathtub use is made from painted squared strip. The "ocean-going" yacht has a modelling medium hull with contrasting portholes and deck. The painted greaseproof paper sails are set on a cocktail stick mast. The boat flies a paper pennant.

A Modern Boy

As he lies on his duvet-covered Scandinavian-style bed, the modern boy can look around him and see the effect of science on his toys and lifestyle. Where his Victorian forebear relied mainly on muscle power and natural materials, today's youngster depends on silicon chips, electricity, batteries, and plastic. His spare time is spent on engaging in sporting events or playing computer games – at which he is a whizz.

Sports equipment The "Louisville slugger" bat and baseball are of modelling medium as are the ice skates.

Telephone and computer The slim-line telephone of modelling medium has plastic spiral cord. The PC's keyboard and monitor also are modelled.

Pin board and basket Paper pin board in mitred wooden frame holds current memorabilia while the paper waste basket holds yesterday's.

Racing set The cars have bead wheels and are directed by handsets to run on the "electrified" oval track. All are made from modelling medium.

Unpainted pine When choosing furniture for a child, pick something that can be self-assembled and is easy to care for. This bed has plain wooden strip sides that can be glued around a cardboard base. The squared strip legs are added last. Foam mattress is topped with fitted sheets and duvet.

THE VICTORIAN BATHROOM

Ornamental cistern is a lace-trimmed rectangular wooden box overpainted with white acrylic

Although it is free of many plumbing restrictions, a doll's house bathroom still must provide scope for its occupants to perform all necessary functions. Today's families often have to make do with only very small bathrooms but Victorian bathrooms, where fitted, were commodious and fixtures were large scale.

A glass-fronted linen cupboard stores freshly starched sheets and fluffy towels; towels in use are kept near at hand on a wooden rail. Beauty and body care supplies are displayed on wall-hung shelves, and shaving supplies in the mirrored cabinet above the sink. The wooden washstand, with shell mirror overhead, houses a hot water bottle, decorative pitcher and basin, soap dish, and dusting powder.

A floral patterned fabric wallcovering is soothing to contemplate while soaking in the bath, and a selection of houseplants – African violets, spider plant, and fern – chosen for enjoying a humid atmosphere, add a touch of greenery displayed on their wooden plant stands.

A folding screen provides the necessary privacy where children about to be bathed can change. The pelmeted window drapes protect the bather from cool breezes while his or her feet are cushioned from the cold marble floor by the woven bath rug.

In case of emergencies, a plunger and pail are within easy reach of the toilet.

A good soak
Mama, at least her capped head and shoulders, lies in a dish washing liquid foam bath and is happy for her few minutes' peace and quiet.

Delicate fern
is created from masking tape and garden wire. See page 9 for instructions

Porcelain and crystal jars
are made from decorative beads. See page 17 for further inspiration

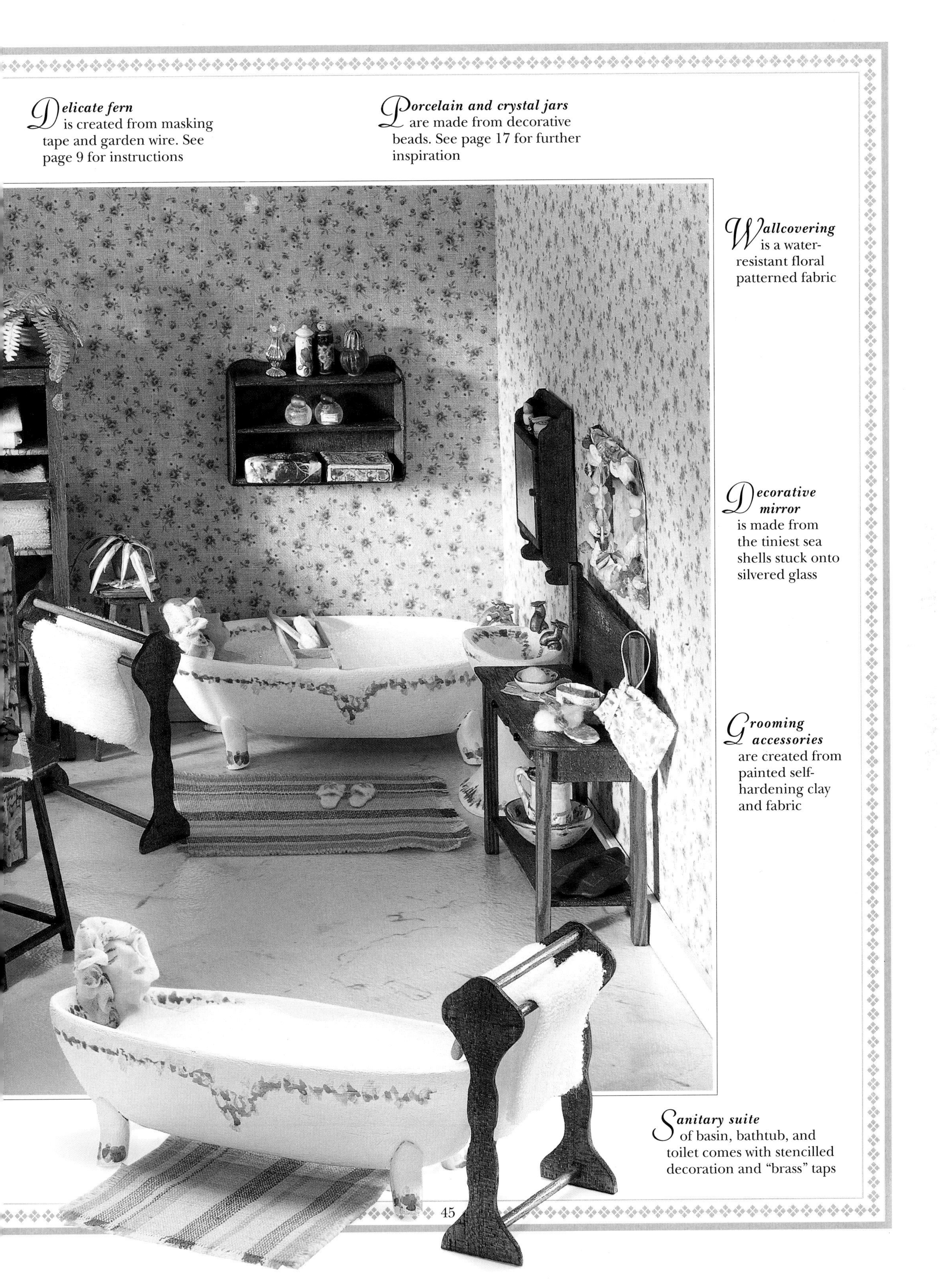

Wallcovering
is a water-resistant floral patterned fabric

Decorative mirror
is made from the tiniest sea shells stuck onto silvered glass

Grooming accessories
are created from painted self-hardening clay and fabric

Sanitary suite
of basin, bathtub, and toilet comes with stencilled decoration and "brass" taps

THE VICTORIAN BATHROOM CATALOGUE

Open cupboard and toiletries
Made of stained and varnished wooden pieces, the cupboard consists of three shelves and two sides fixed to a curved back. A range of perfumes and body lotions, in jars of crystal beads, are arrayed on the shelves. The storage boxes are small blocks of wood covered with wrapping paper.

Bath accessories
Glued wood strips, cotton wool, embroidery thread, and natural sponge can be used to make an assortment of useful items such as the draining platform, bath tray, washing sponges, and back and nail brushes.

Spider plant and violets
Long leaves are masking tape on fine fuse wire (see page 9) while the smaller leaves and pots are of self-hardening clay.

Toilet roll holder and hooks
These are made from pieces of varnished wood and one or more golden-headed pins. Thin metal wire is bent around the toilet paper, carefully cut from tissues and rolled up.

Fabric items
The dressing gown with matching cap is made from cotton remnants. A floral pattern suits the toilet bag, while the mules and moccasins are of felt with masking tape soles. A swatch of striped fabric suited the bath mat. Fringe is created by pulling some threads from the sides.

Plunger and pail
A cocktail-stick handle and modelled cap make the plunger; templates for the pail are on page 66.

Dusting powder set
The box is floral paper fixed to circular shapes; the puff is cotton wool.

Gentleman's cupboard
Complete with foil mirror and beaded handle this shelved, varnished wooden unit contains all the shaving gear a man could crave. Shaving soap and badger brush of modelling medium accompany silver-painted modelled razors.

Scented soaps
Welcomed by all dolls' house residents and guests, a selection of perfumed favourites are created from beads, or balls of modelling medium, covered with tissue paper and a decorative seal. Finely patterned floral papers are wrapped around rectangular wooden blocks and/or cardboard shapes for the boxes and lids.

Washing accessories
The "china" pitcher, basin, and soap dishes are essential to the Victorian doll's toilette. Shaped self-hardening clay is gaily painted and used to house balls of soap.

Hot water bottles
Made of modelling medium, the delineated patterns are incised with a sharp tool before baking.

Wall and shaving mirrors
Real mirror has shells stuck to it for a decorative border. Foil makes a mirrored front to a metal blazer button fixed to a cardboard base.

Linens and towel rack
Remnants of terry towelling, broderie Anglaise, and striped sheeting are used to suggest their real-life cousins. Thin strips of ribbon duplicate the niceties of items stored in Victorian linen cupboards. The towel rack is constructed from templates shown on page 70.

THE VICTORIAN BATHROOM FURNITURE

Small Square Table

A match to the one found in the sitting room, this small table can be used to hold guests' soaps and towels or assorted reading material. Instructions and templates for table are on page 80.

Fabric Screen

To ensure modesty, lengths of fabric, stiffened with wallpaper paste, are gathered within wood strips. Full making-up instructions on page 80.

Modelling medium African violets in self-hardening clay pots

Fabric is pleated and stiffened with wallpaper paste

Rub-down transfer provides gold-leaf ornamentation

Doily cut from lacy material

Pitcher and bowl of self-hardening clay

Plant Stand

Ideal for holding indoor plants, the instructions and templates for making this unit with integral shelf are on page 70.

Wooden Washstand

Created from wood strip and stained the appropriate colour, this has bead handles and a transfer decoration. Between two 10 cm (4 in) pieces of 6 mm (1/4 in) squared strip, glue the 75 x 40 mm (3 x 1 9/16 in) back. Cut two 65mm (2 9/16 in) pieces of squared strip for front legs and between them and back legs, attach two 22 x 10 mm (7/8 x 3/8 in) side pieces cut from wood strip. Add a front 6 mm (1/4 in) wide between the two front legs and attach two smaller "drawer" fronts. Cut a 34 x 80 mm (1 1/4 x 3 1/8 in) bottom shelf, notching the corners and glue to bottom legs. Add a 40 x 85 mm (1 9/16 x 3 5/16 in) top, cutting a square piece out of both back corners to fit between back legs. Add transfer decoration and bead knobs.

Linen Cupboard

A variation of the wardrobe on page 40, this 10 x 15 x 4 cm (4 x 6 x 1½ in) rectanglar cupboard is constructed from 2 sides, a back, and a top of wood strip. Adapt the templates on page 74 but use the door pattern found on page 75. Strips of clear plastic are attached behind the wooden frame to form the "glass" front. There are four interior shelves; the bottom one forms the base. The top three are covered in paper. Brass hinges, cut from gold tape, and gold beads provide the trim. The top has a decorative curved moulding, roughly cut from wood then shaped by sandpaper wrapped around a pencil. All visible pieces are stained.

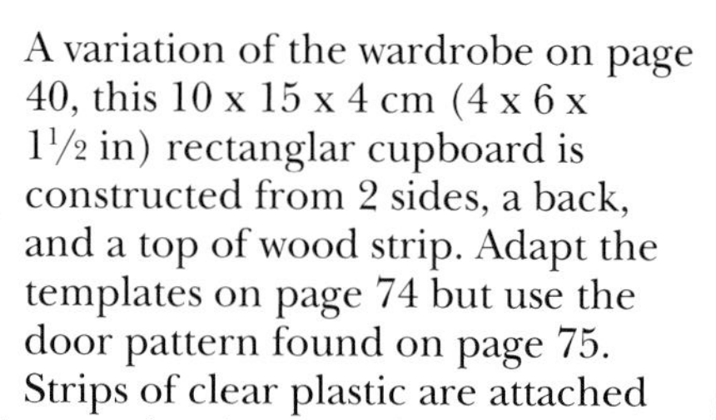

"Relief" decoration is painted lace

Cistern and Toilet

The toilet, made from self-hardening clay painted with white acrylic, is decorated with "stencilling" and has a wooden-effect clay seat. It is attached to the cistern by means of a white-painted dowel, which is fixed to it with a wad of plastic adhesive. The cistern, a 25 x 40 x 23 mm (1 x 1$^{9}/_{16}$ x $^{7}/_{8}$ in) white-painted wooden rectangle has a lace "relief" trim.

Wooden toilet seat is self-hardening clay painted brown

Head and shoulders only need to be modelled

Linens and towels are miniature versions of the real thing

Wash Basin

To match the rest of the sanitary ware, this pedestal wash basin, made from self-hardening clay, is heavily stencilled and has "brass" taps made from modelling medium. It has a tiny modelled plug, which is used to stop up the gold-painted drain, and it is fitted to a freely movable thin chain.

Jewellery chain holds modelled plug

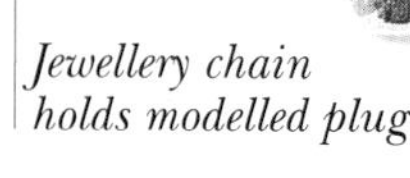

Footed Bath

Made of self-hardening clay, this ample bath has a white acrylic paint finish, "brass" modelling medium taps and a "stencilled" trim. A modelled plug is attached to a thin chain to keep the tub filled with water.

THE MODERN BATHROOM

Smaller, warmer, and more efficient than its Victorian counterpart, the bathroom of today's modern doll contains numerous aids to beauty, as well as a wealth of boxed and bottled items that contribute to personal care. One result of modern plumbing expertise is that the old washstand with its china bowls and pitcher have been replaced by a modern sink with hot and cold running water, and the cast iron bath has been superseded by a pulsating shower unit in curtained ceramic stall. They may be less impressive visually, but certainly more hygienic.

Toilet rolls
Pastel-shaded papers are cut from paper tissues and wound on drinking-straw cores. Painted wood and metal wire form the holder.

Electrical beauty aids
Portable hair dryers, heated curlers, and an electric razor are some modern modelled essentials.

Hot water bottle
This modelled rectangle has a felt-tip patterned fabric covering and a modelled leak-proof stopper.

Towels
An assortment of bath and hand towels are created from remnants of fine terry towelling – the type used for baby stretch suits. They are dyed in a small batch of food colouring. The modern towel rail is fixed to the wall, not free-standing, and is made of white-painted wood and thin dowel.

Essential make-up
A tiny zippered pouch contains a supply of modelled lipsticks, nail varnish, and mascara, and bead eye shadow.

Hair care items
Brushes, combs, and hair bands can be stored in the basket when not in use. All are made from modelling medium.

Bath-time toys
A school of fish, a trio of ducks, and a simple tug are fashioned out of modelling medium.

Tooth care A set of brushes – one for each member of the family, a mug, and tooth paste are all created from modelling medium.

Bathroom scale Two modelled rectangles of differing sizes are glued one on top of the other. The calibrations can be inked in or cut from paper and covered with a circle of plastic. For comfort, felt fabric is glued to the top.

Assorted soaps Plain beauty bars, small guests' soaps, and soaps on a rope are modern-day essentials. Modelling medium and thread are all that is needed.

Bath sponges Both natural and artificial sponges are cut to form appropriate shapes. The "loofah" has threads attached to enable its user to apply it to those hard-to-get-at places.

Accessories shelf A wooden unit stores the perfumes, creams, lotions, and paper products preferred by today's doll. Most items are modelled.

Cover and mat set Stretchable terry towelling fabric, in a coordinating shade to the towels, is used for the three-piece suite. The choice of today's modern home-maker, this consists of a toilet lid cover, cut-to-fit toilet mat, and bath mat.

En Suite Shower Room

Where space is a problem, a shower room often can be installed where a full-sized bathroom won't fit. As long as a toilet can be sited elsewhere, sanitary regulations won't prevent the shower and sink-and-storage unit being fitted into the master bedroom.

THE VICTORIAN

Sitting Room

This, the grandest room in the house, must also be a model of comfort and relaxed domesticity. Papa retreats here when he wants to leave the hustle and bustle of family life behind.

The decor is somewhat formal – no expense has been spared for the elegant striped wallpaper, pelmeted drapes, and needlepoint carpets. Hanging pictures on a ribbon band, such as the flower prints displayed here, is a popular decorative device.

The furniture is also substantial. The glass-fronted cabinet contains ornaments off-limits to children. The green-seated side chair and the desk and matching chair are of good sturdy oak. More lavish are the fringed velvet settee and brocade wing chair.

A number of accessories also attest to the relative prosperity of the inhabitants: the Staffordshire dogs, antique china wall plates, corner collection of "Moss ware", and the variety of gilt-framed oil paintings. In keeping with nineteenth-century convention, Mama has placed all her "best" items here to impress her visitors.

Comfort has been catered for with the satin scatter cushions plumped up on the settee, the needlepointed footstool, the smokers' accessories, and the welcoming display of fresh fruits and sugared plums in their milk glass bowls on their circular table.

Mama's touch is clearly apparent in the selection of fresh flowers and plants scattered throughout the room. The pot pourri on the crocheted tablecloth helps to dispel the fumes of any of Papa's cigar-smoking friends.

Ancestral portraits are real photographs cut down and placed in plaited frames

Garden roses of modelling medium are freshly gathered in modelled jug

Velvet drapes
are fixed to a cardboard pelmet covered with fringe

Framed prints
can be easily reproduced using stamps and mitred wooden pieces. Full directions are given on page 13

Potted plants
are easily made from masking tape and wire. Follow the directions on page 9

Ornamental china
made of self-hardening clay is easy to create; see page 11

Petit point rug
is quickly stitched using a rectangle of canvas and silken or cotton threads

Papa's corner
Although Moma had a free hand with the rest of the room, Papa insisted on having his old desk and smoking paraphernalia near at hand in the sitting room.

THE VICTORIAN SITTING ROOM CATALOGUE

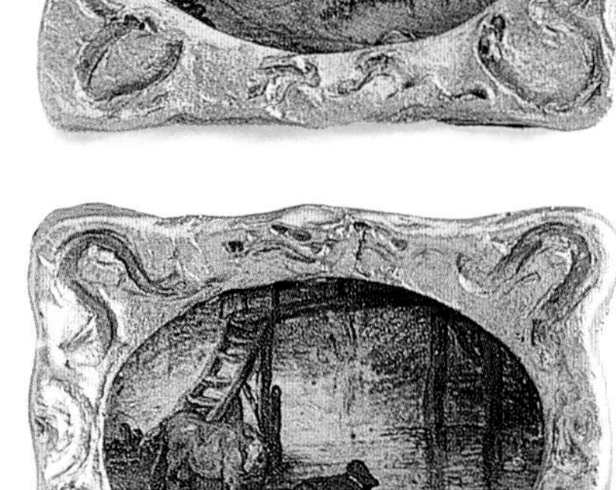

Fabric frames Victorian wall treatments made much use of ribbon. Here, photographs of family forebears are framed in fabric braid that is offset by bows. Ribbon streamers are used to display paper ovals with dried flower motifs.

Smoking accoutrements A box of cigars, a humidor, and a tobacco canister accompany the floor-standing ashtray. All but the box are of brown modelling medium decorated with gold paint.

Gilt frames Pastoral scenes, found in magazines or on greetings cards, are offset by frame-shaped, incised self-hardening clay painted gold.

Frames and doily The tiniest of images are glued to cardboard backs and framed by silver plastic modelling material; they sit on a scrap of lacy fabric.

Staffordshire china Ubiquitous figurines, here of self-hardening clay, can grace shelves and mantlepieces.

Scatter cushions Scraps of satin fabric are gathered around tufts of wadding and stitched. Tiny floral motifs provide the finishing touch; see page 15 for tips.

Desk accessories Essential reference tomes, made of papered-over wood, aid the writer in search of the perfect phrase. The paper blotter has ribbon corners, the pens are modelled, the stamp box is wood and the letter file is paper.

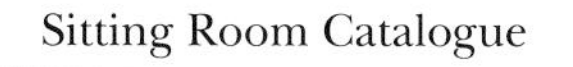

Fruits and chocolates
Sugar-coated plums, fresh fruit in a basket, and boxed chocolates are of modelling medium and paper.

Decorative plates
Self-hardening clay is shaped into circles and then gaily painted in patterns reminiscent of the 18th century. Then, as now, they were used to decorate walls. See page 11 for how-to.

Butterfly collection
Framed in stained and varnished wood, the paper insects, carefully cut from a magazine advertisement, are a lepidopterist's delight.

Wall clock
A button forms the face and a paper fastener acts as the pendulum. Thin strips of gold tape are used to decorate the wooden case.

Plants and flowers
Masking tape and garden wire aspidistra, and dried and modelled flowers are displayed in a cloisonné bead vase.

Wooden whatnot
Instructions and templates for this decorative corner display unit with triangular shelves are on page 80. The "Moss ware" is porcelain modelling medium.

Roses
Modelled blooms on garden wire stalks repose in modelled basket near pot pourri petals.

Needlepoint items
A rectangle of canvas covered in diamonds of petit point makes the ideal carpet. The footstool is a rectangular wooden box on bead feet. A floral petit point cover surrounds a pillow of wadding that fits the frame.

THE VICTORIAN SITTING ROOM FURNITURE

CIRCULAR TABLE

This cardboard table is constructed exactly the same as its full-size cousins. Full making-up instructions on page 72.

Sturdy velvet fabric topped with lace provides appropriate period feel

CURIO CABINET

The back of this cardboard cabinet is a 65 x 112 mm ($2^1/_2$ x $4^7/_{16}$ in) rectangle. To it glue two sides, each 25 x 100 mm (1 x 4 in). Glue on rectangle for the top. Apply foil to the inside of the cabinet and to the tops of three shelves. Position one shelf on the bottom to hold the feet then glue all in place. Cut two doors using the template on page 75. Attach doors by masking tape "hinges" on the side; add bead knobs, and four 6 mm ($^1/_4$ in) lengths of squared strip for the legs.

Carefully carved fretwork pattern

"Mirrored" shelves and sides created by foil

Knobs are irridescent beads

WING-BACK CHAIR

Deeply padded seat, back, and arms covered in hard-wearing floral print offers durable comfort. Templates and instructions are on page 70.

OCCASIONAL CHAIR

This is simple to construct out of cardboard, modelling medium, wadding, and fabric. For the seat, form a cardboard rectangular box, 50 mm (2in) at the front tapering to 45 mm ($1^3/_4$ in) at the rear, 40 mm ($1^1/_2$ in) deep and with 12 mm ($^1/_2$ in) sides. Add wadding to top then cover with fabric, tucking in ends. Cover another piece of card, the same dimensions as the seat top, with fabric and glue to bottom of seat to neaten bottom and provide a base for legs.

Cut a rectangular back 65 x 40 mm ($2^1/_2$ x $1^1/_2$ in). Cover the front with wadding and then fabric. Glue the padded side of the back to the seat. Apply ribbon along the seat edge and add four modelled legs.

Create legs from modelling medium

Wooden Desk

Essential for holding all the important family papers, this is easy to make out of wood strip, single-ply plywood, and gold-headed pins. Cut the back, a 125 x 65 mm (5 x 2 9/16 in) rectangle, and two interior drawer sides, 60 x 65 mm (2 3/8 x 2 9/16 in) rectangles, out of plywood. Cut two exterior drawer sides, a 125 x 62 mm (5 x 2 3/8 in) top, and two 38 x 67 mm (1 1/2 x 2 5/8 in) fronts out of woodstrip. Stain all pieces as desired.

When dry, rough assemble and then glue the two exterior sides to the back. Carefully position the two interior sides and glue these to the back, then add the fronts and top. Cut six 15 x 30 mm (5/16 x 1 3/16 in) drawer fronts out of wood strip and glue three to each front. Push pins through the wood to form knobs.

Inkwells of crystal beads

Push pins through to form drawer pulls

Small Square Table

Useful as an occasional table in a variety of places around the house, to hold plants and photographs, for example, the instructions for this simple table are on page 80.

Wooden Chair

Coated in matching stain to desk, this is made with the templates and instructions on page 80.

Arms, back, and seat are thickly padded

Chocolates of modelling medium nestle in gilt-paper covered box

Settee

A sofa you can sink into, this plush piece of furniture takes pride of place in any sitting room. The fringed trim and beaded feet are in proper period style. Full making-up instructions are on page 71.

THE 1930'S SITTING ROOM

The decorator planning to recreate this look should bear in mind the influences on the period – which were new directions in design and a stagnating economy. Art Deco designers favoured geometric detailing on wood, the malleable properties of plastic, and bright patterns on ceramics. The economies of the period meant that hand-knitted and embroidered goods often had to take the place of commercially produced ones.

Gift parcels
Filled with hand-knitted socks and gloves these paper-wrapped wood boxes are tied with thread twine.

Susie Cooper tea set
Teapot, cups and saucers, sugar bowl, and milk jug are made of self-hardening clay. See page 11 for tips on making.

Knitting accessories
Cocktail-stick needles with bead handles are used to knit skeins of embroidery-thread yarn. The needles and yarn are kept safe from prying hands in embroidered felt carryalls.

Photograph album
Paper leaves hold "photographs" of relatives past and present cut from stamps, magazines, and catalogues. The "leatherbound" cover is made of cardboard trimmed with paper.

Home sweet home
Embroidered picture, is done in diagonal stitch with single thread on petit point canvas. See page 13 for framing tips.

Deco clock
Graduated rectangles of wood strip are glued to a central block. The face is from a magazine.

Thirties plates
Self-hardening clay plates are painted with period decoration. See page 11 for how-to.

Domestic Bliss

A haven against growing monetary and political problems, the '30s sitting room epitomizes comfortable domesticity. Thoughts of relatives are ever present, witness the gift parcels ready for posting and the well thumbed family photograph album. The radio is a constant companion along with one's knitting, and there is always the sweet trolley when worries become too pressing.

Thirties radios
The "carved wood" cardboard façades fit over mesh "speakers" and plastic tuning bands. "Bakelite" knobs are beads.

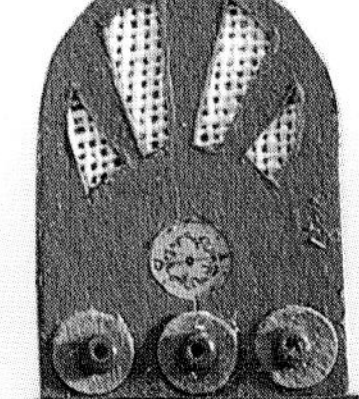

Pipes and tobacco
Carved wooden pipe-rack supports a selection while the felt tobacco pouch holds a pinch of the real thing. Cocktail-stick cleaners, painted white, are on hand to clear any obstructions.

Magazine rack
Made from cardboard it holds various publications of paper, or wood blocks covered in printed illustrations.

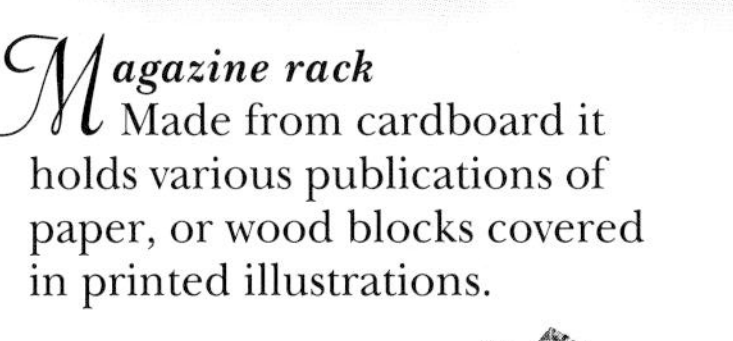

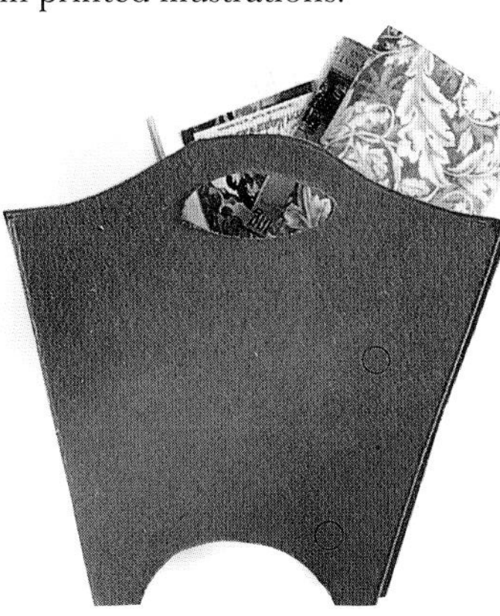

Decorative "barbola" mirror
Plasticized foil has cardboard backing and painted modelled trim. It hangs by jewellery chain.

Comfy cushions
Made for use on floors and sofas, squares of plain and plush material are filled with millet or other seeds. Alternatively, plain fabric can be decorated with embroidered flowers and trimmed in chain stitch before filling.

The Family

An entire family of dolls can be created simply from modelling medium; pipe cleaners; surgical tape; strong, clear adhesive, and fabric. The head and limbs are modelled then baked according to the manufacturer's instructions. When dry, the body is assembled and can be clothed. Add a few sprigs of lavender to make them scented. Faces can be modelled as desired. Facial features are painted on and may require some practice on paper before you become proficient. With brown paint make the eyebrows and outline the eyes. When dry, add irises then touches of white for the corner, and finally add further brown for eyelashes and to accentuate any features. Paint mouth red or pink.

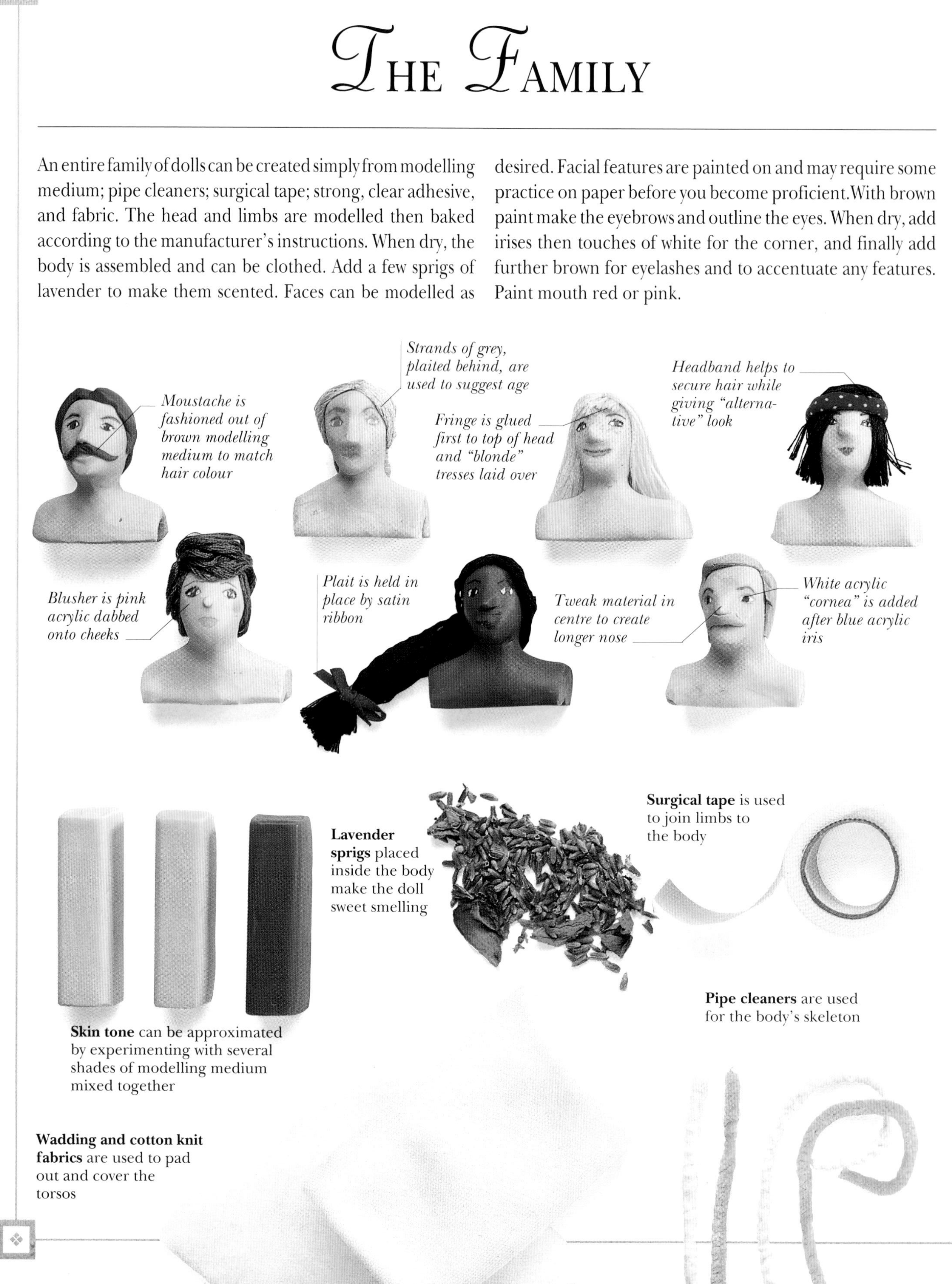

Moustache is fashioned out of brown modelling medium to match hair colour

Strands of grey, plaited behind, are used to suggest age

Fringe is glued first to top of head and "blonde" tresses laid over

Headband helps to secure hair while giving "alternative" look

Blusher is pink acrylic dabbed onto cheeks

Plait is held in place by satin ribbon

Tweak material in centre to create longer nose

White acrylic "cornea" is added after blue acrylic iris

Lavender sprigs placed inside the body make the doll sweet smelling

Surgical tape is used to join limbs to the body

Pipe cleaners are used for the body's skeleton

Skin tone can be approximated by experimenting with several shades of modelling medium mixed together

Wadding and cotton knit fabrics are used to pad out and cover the torsos

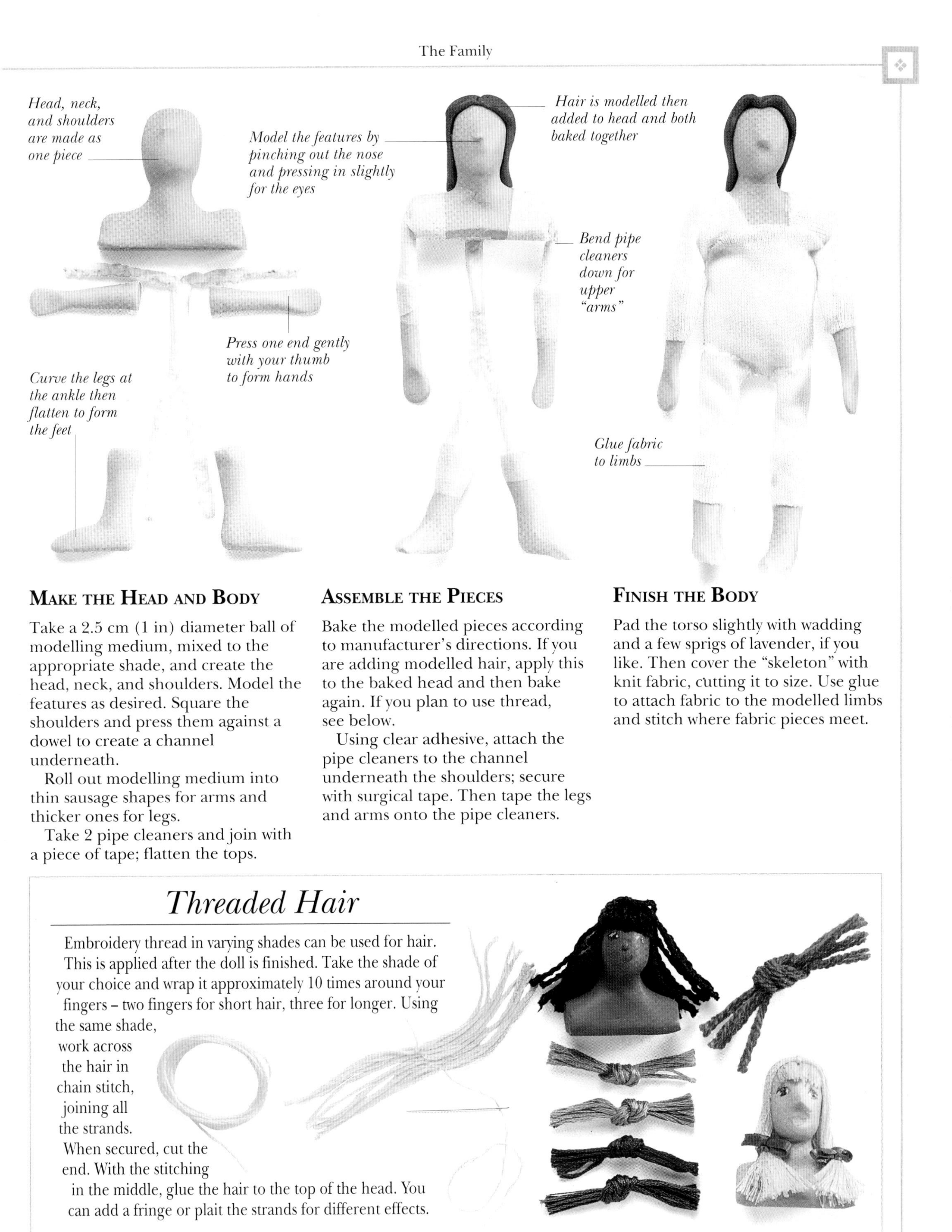

Head, neck, and shoulders are made as one piece

Model the features by pinching out the nose and pressing in slightly for the eyes

Hair is modelled then added to head and both baked together

Bend pipe cleaners down for upper "arms"

Press one end gently with your thumb to form hands

Curve the legs at the ankle then flatten to form the feet

Glue fabric to limbs

Make the Head and Body

Take a 2.5 cm (1 in) diameter ball of modelling medium, mixed to the appropriate shade, and create the head, neck, and shoulders. Model the features as desired. Square the shoulders and press them against a dowel to create a channel underneath.

Roll out modelling medium into thin sausage shapes for arms and thicker ones for legs.

Take 2 pipe cleaners and join with a piece of tape; flatten the tops.

Assemble the Pieces

Bake the modelled pieces according to manufacturer's directions. If you are adding modelled hair, apply this to the baked head and then bake again. If you plan to use thread, see below.

Using clear adhesive, attach the pipe cleaners to the channel underneath the shoulders; secure with surgical tape. Then tape the legs and arms onto the pipe cleaners.

Finish the Body

Pad the torso slightly with wadding and a few sprigs of lavender, if you like. Then cover the "skeleton" with knit fabric, cutting it to size. Use glue to attach fabric to the modelled limbs and stitch where fabric pieces meet.

Threaded Hair

Embroidery thread in varying shades can be used for hair. This is applied after the doll is finished. Take the shade of your choice and wrap it approximately 10 times around your fingers – two fingers for short hair, three for longer. Using the same shade, work across the hair in chain stitch, joining all the strands. When secured, cut the end. With the stitching in the middle, glue the hair to the top of the head. You can add a fringe or plait the strands for different effects.

Dressing the Family

While it is perfectly possible to make clothes from patterns, the simplest and most effective way of dressing the family is to cut scraps of fabric and, using a strong clear adhesive, glue them directly to the doll. Solids or small print fabrics work best. To prevent the edges of certain materials unravelling, use a commercially available fray preventer or clear nail varnish. Materials should be made of natural fibres as these drape more readily and effectively than polyesters or acrylics.

Hair and earrings are glued to the head, if not modelled, and shoes can be painted on the feet, if desired.

Stitch sides of waistcoat after dressing figure

Wrap material around leg then stitch inner seams

Trousers and waistcoat are simple shapes that are tailored to fit and then glued

Dressing a Man

Trousers and tops are applied directly over integral long johns. While the shirt consists of a separate back, front, and sleeves, the waistcoat and flannel trousers are both cleverly cut from one piece of fabric. The trousers are wrapped around the legs and the inner seams are stitched. The waistcoat is placed over the head and the outer seams are stitched.

Dressing a Woman

Normally, attire is made up of several pieces. A petticoat, of broderie anglaise, is made first and applied directly over the integral underwear. Then the sleeves and bodice of the dress are attached, followed by the gathered skirt. Finally lace or other trim is added.

Dress is made in several pieces. The sleeves and back are attached first, then the gathered skirt, and finally the front with lace collar is added. The petticoat, of broderie anglaise, was made first

Trims neaten and adorn garments

A single garment may be made up of a number of pieces

Costume Gallery

Babies wear nappies of terry towelling and christening dress of lace fabric over white satin

Victorian housemaid sports an apron and cap over everyday shift of striped fabric

Hair is modelled and the moustache and shoes painted on afterwards

Victorian man wears satin smoking jacket and cravat with cotton trousers

Victorian woman wears a frock of satin trimmed with plaid. Her hat is made from a matching fabric scrap and feather

Earrings are tiny jewellery findings glued to her head

Teenager is dressed in knitted top and corduroy trousers

Adolescent boy with freckle-fresh face sports woven jeans and checked shirt

Girl wears small print dress with pinafore of lacy material. Her strappy shoes are painted on

Country woman is dressed in calico dress with homespun apron on top. Her straw hat is made from plaited threads

Using the Templates

The templates will produce furniture that is of $^1/_{12}$th scale. Do not cut the templates from the book but use tracing paper to create a paper template and transfer this to wood or cardboard. Be careful to transfer the score lines properly; a straight-edge will come in handy. It is recommended to rough assemble all pieces first to make sure of fit, so that if anything isn't exact you can adjust for it before glueing. Remember, too, to stain any wood pieces before you apply the glue.

Occasionally you may want to enlarge a template to suit a doll larger than the $^1/_{12}$th size, a model doll, for example. Or, you may want to reduce a larger pattern, found in another book, for use in your doll's house. The instructions given on the opposite page are easy to follow but a good result depends upon accurate measuring and correct positioning.

To reduce a larger pattern or template, follow the procedure for enlarging but reverse the process so you work from the greater measure to the lesser.

You will find the necessary instructions to complete each item near its set of templates. In addition to the list of supplies given, scissors or a craft knife will be needed to cut (and score) the templates.

Some of the templates need to be used more than once in constructing a particular item, and will be marked "Cut 2", for example.

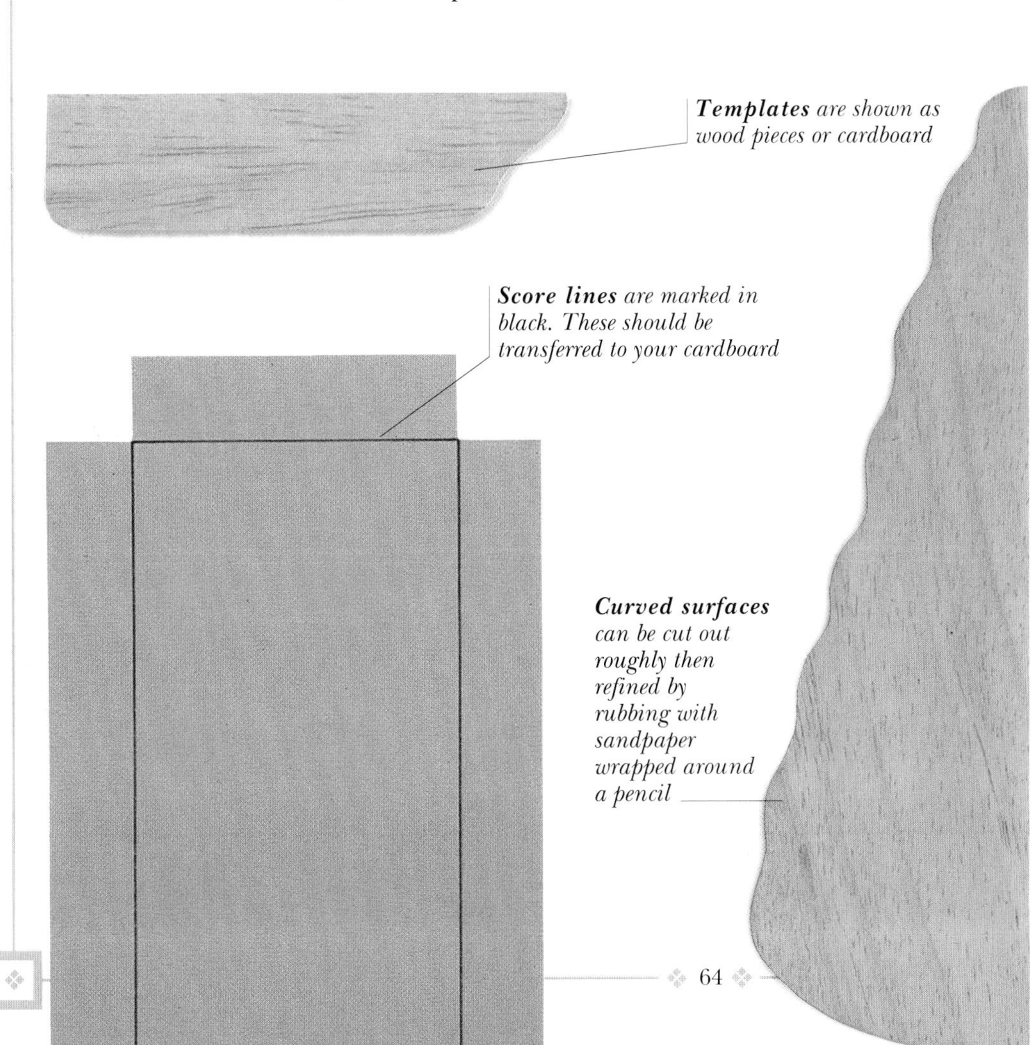

Templates *are shown as wood pieces or cardboard*

Score lines *are marked in black. These should be transferred to your cardboard*

Curved surfaces *can be cut out roughly then refined by rubbing with sandpaper wrapped around a pencil*

Index to Templates/ Instructions

Enlarging a Template

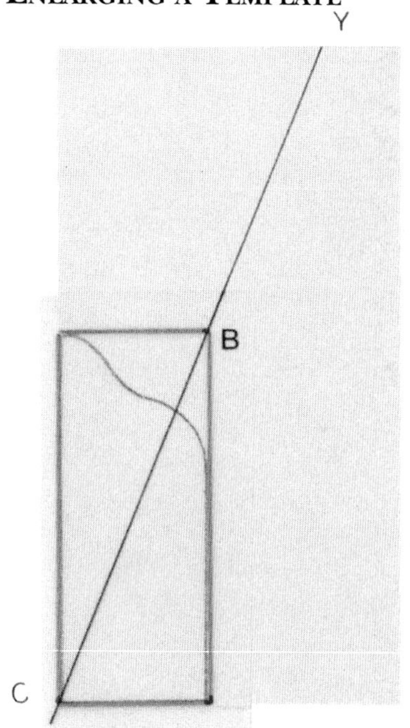

1 ~ Trace the template and draw a rectangle around it. Then take a large piece of paper and lay the traced template at the corner of it. Draw a line from the bottom left (C) through the top right (B) and onwards to the the larger piece (Y).

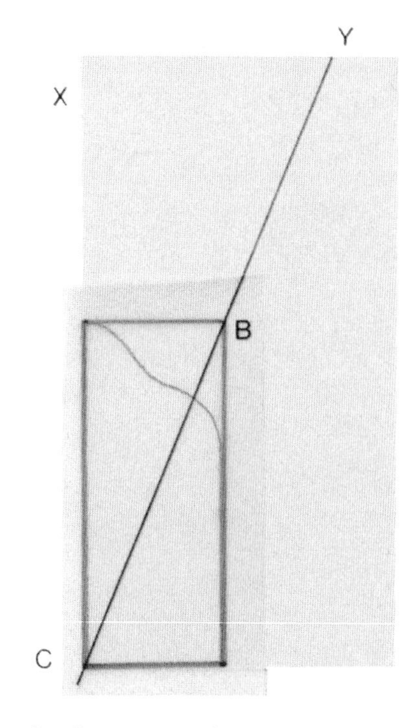

2 ~ Determine the desired height of the enlargement by working upwards from the bottom left (C) and to your chosen point. Mark this with an X.

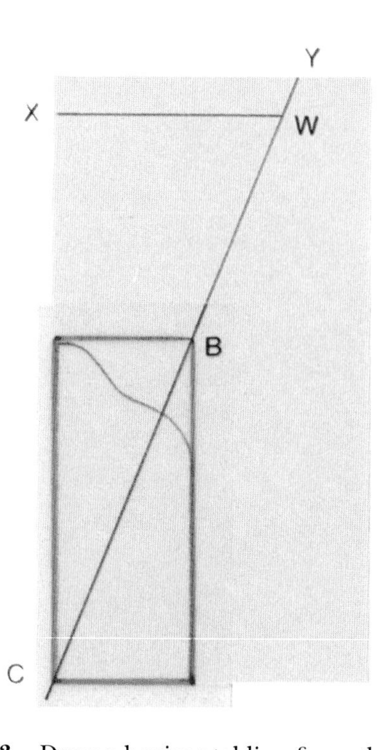

3 ~ Draw a horizontal line from the point (X) of the larger paper through line CBY to (W), the right-hand point, making sure it is parallel to the base.

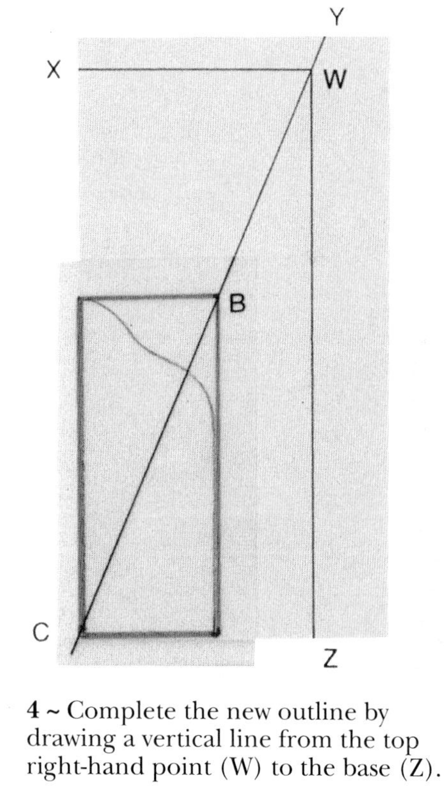

4 ~ Complete the new outline by drawing a vertical line from the top right-hand point (W) to the base (Z).

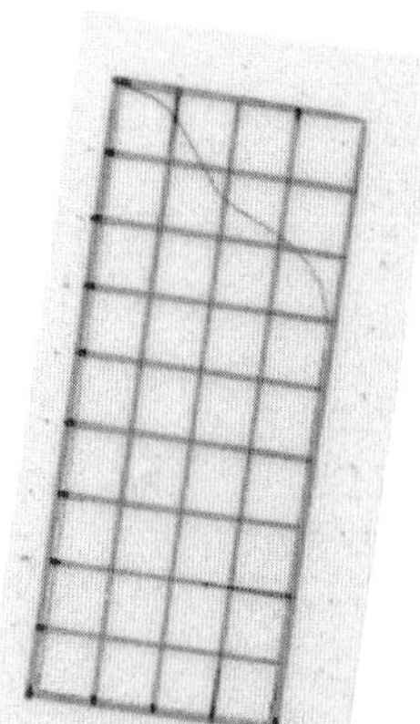

5 ~ Divide the original template and the new outline into the same number of squares. Draw the template freehand, square by square, on the new outline with its proportionally larger squares, using a ruler for a straight edge.

Dressing Table

You will need ~
Traces of 2 templates
Cardboard
Tape
Fabric
Glue
Lace trim
Decorative ribbon

1 ~ Transfer template traces to cardboard. For pedestal bases, score along black lines and fold into rectangles, holding the corners together with tape.

2 ~ Cover with fabric, stuck on with glue. Add lace trim to the bottom of each base.

3 ~ For table top, score along black lines and fold; tape the corners.

4 ~ Cover with fabric then apply lace all around the perimeter of the top. Add decorative ribbon trim around edges.

5 ~ Using glue, attach the pedestals to the table top.

Pedestal base
Cut 2

Fold along lines

Dressing table top
Cut 1

Fold along lines

Pail

You will need ~
Traces of 2 templates
Paper
Glue
Silver paint
Fuse wire

1 ~ Transfer the traces to paper and assemble the pail by wrapping the larger piece onto itself so that the 2 handle supports are opposite each other. Glue the join.

2 ~ Push the bottom piece inside and paint the pail with silver.

3 ~ Thread fuse wire through hole in each handle support; bend the end up.

Pail
Cut 1

Bottom
Cut 1

Fuse wire

Shelf

You will need ~
Traces of 3 templates
Wood strip
Tea for stain, optional
Masking tape
Glue

1 ~ Transfer traces of templates to wood strip and cut out the back piece, two sides, and three shelves.

2 ~ For "pine" effect, stain with tea, 2 or 3 coats may be necessary.

3 ~ Glue the side pieces to the back and position the shelves, using masking tape, to check fit.

4 ~ When you are happy with the fit, glue the shelves to the sides and back.

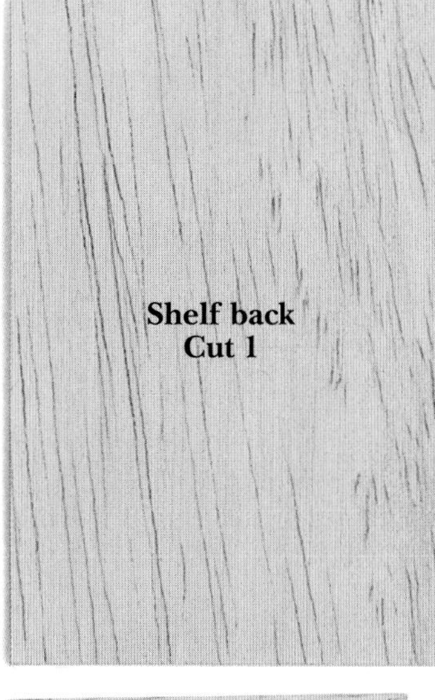

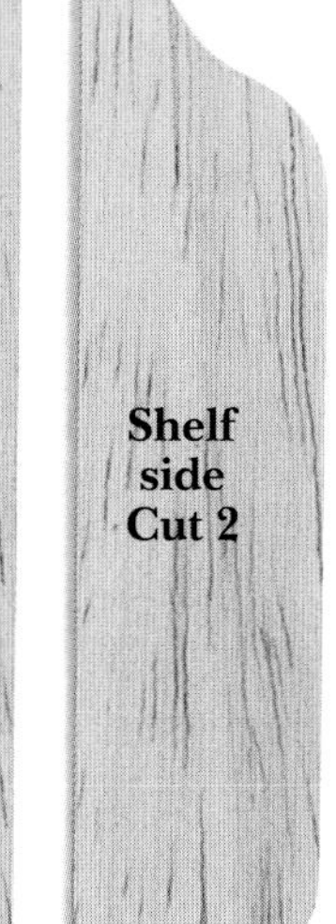

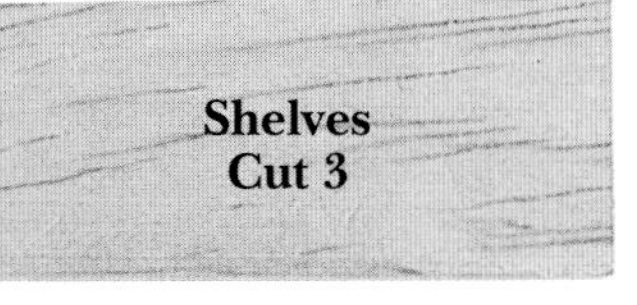

Bathtub Rack

Side Cut 2

You will need ~
Traces of 3 templates
Wood strip
Glue

Side Cut 2

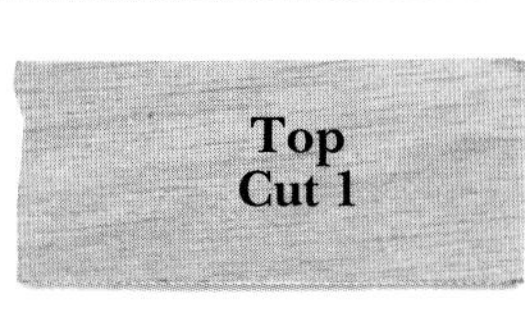

1 ~ Transfer traces of templates to wood and cut top and 4 sides. Use emery board or sandpaper wrapped around a pencil to neaten curves.

2 ~ Glue sides together then attach top.

Serving Trolley

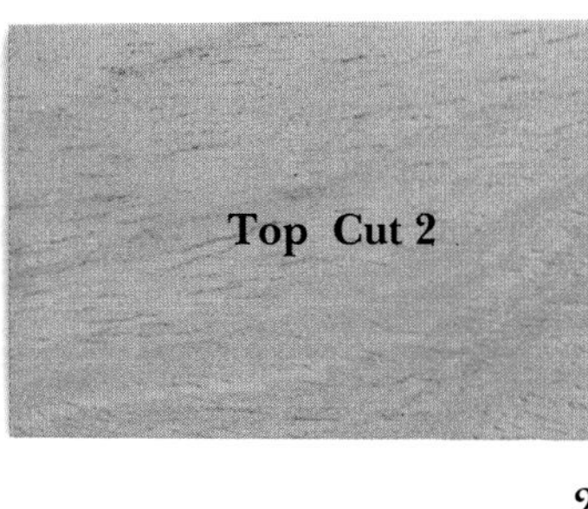

You will need ~
Traces of 1 template
Squared strip
Wood strip
Wood stain
Glue
4 paper fasteners

1 ~ Transfer trace to wood strip and cut out 2 tops.

2 ~ Out of squared strip cut 8 sides to lengths shown. Cut 4 legs 6 mm (1/4 in) longer than longest side.

3 ~ Stain all pieces; when dry, glue sides to tops and then glue legs.

4 ~ Remove one end of fasteners, leaving head for wheel and push other end into bottom of leg.

Side Cut 4

Paper fastener

Side Cut 4

Sewing Box

You will need ~
Traces of 6 templates
Wood strip
Squared strip
Stain
Glue
Lace
Brown paper

1 ~ Transfer traced templates to wood and cut top, base, cross piece, 2 legs, and 4 sides. Cut 4 feet and 2 supports from squared strip to lengths shown. Cut 4 dividers from brown paper.

2 ~ With sandpaper wrapped round a pencil, smooth the curves in the legs. Trim the perimeter of the box with a strip of lace cut to size and stain along with wood.

3 ~ When pieces are dry, join the sides to the underneath of the base and glue on the supports. Then add the legs and graduated feet. Slot in the cross piece at the bottom between the graduated feet.

4 ~ Cut notches in the paper dividers at one-third and two-thirds along their lengths and fit together to form nine compartments.

5 ~ If you like, you can decorate the top of the box.

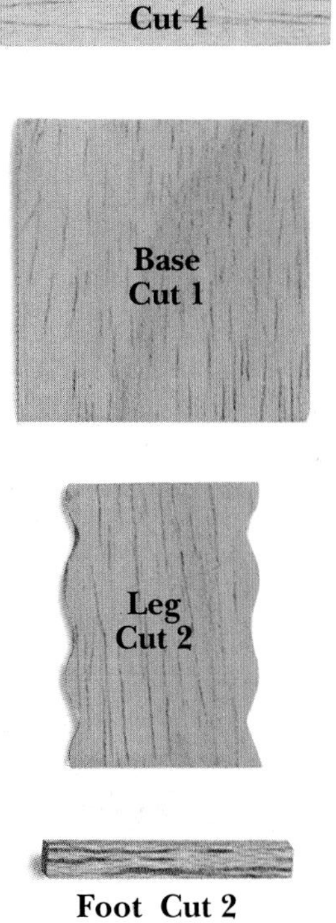

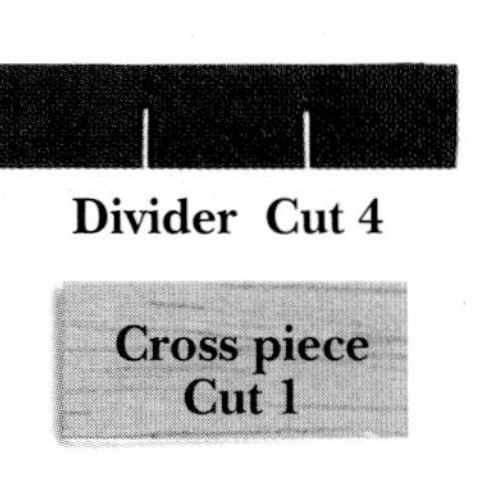

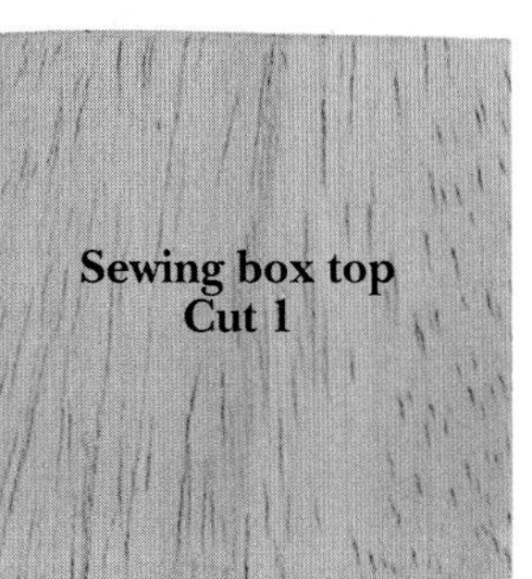

Foot Cut 2

Support Cut 2

Foot Cut 2

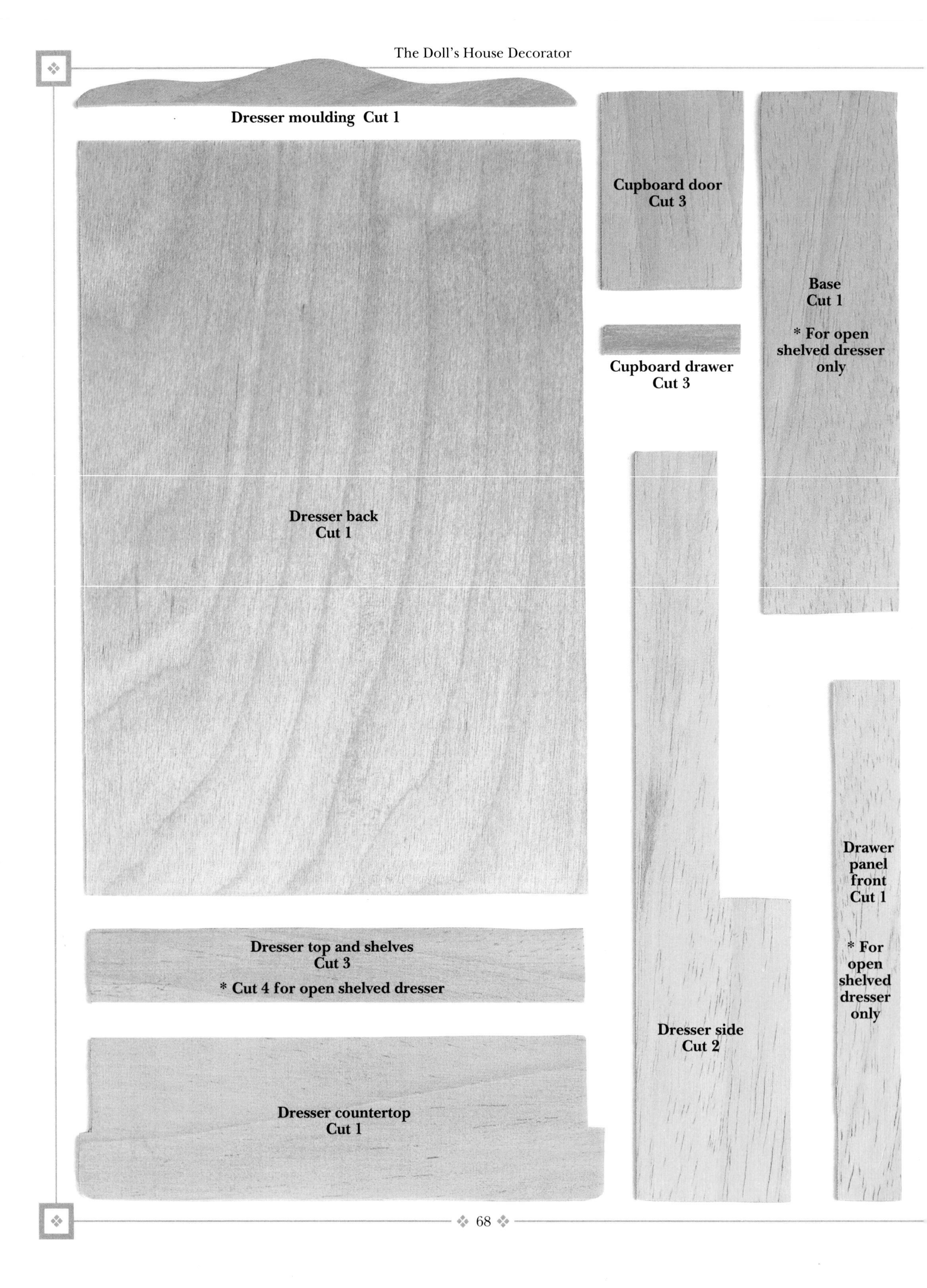
Dresser moulding Cut 1
Dresser back
Cut 1
Cupboard door
Cut 3
Cupboard drawer
Cut 3
Base
Cut 1
* For open
shelved dresser
only
Dresser top and shelves
Cut 3
* Cut 4 for open shelved dresser
Dresser countertop
Cut 1
Dresser side
Cut 2
Drawer
panel
front
Cut 1
* For
open
shelved
dresser
only

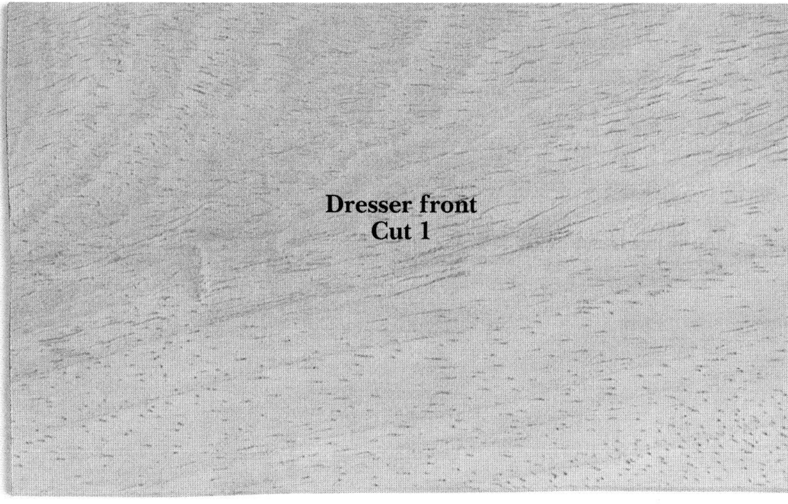

Welsh Dresser

You will need ~
Traces of 8 templates
Wood strip
Single-ply plywood
Masking tape
Glue
Modelling medium
Tea for stain, optional

1 ~ Transfer traces of template shapes for the 2 sides, 2 shelves and top, countertop, 3 cupboard doors, 3 drawers, curved moulding, and front to the wood strip. Cut out shapes. Cut out back from plywood.

2 ~ Using masking tape, rough assemble the major pieces – the two sides to the back, and the front to the sides. Slot in the shelves and the top and countertop.

3 ~ When you are happy with the fit, if you like, remove the tape and stain all the pieces with strong tea, 2 or 3 coats may be necessary.

4 ~ When the pieces are dry, glue all pieces together adding the curved moulding, the cupboard doors, and the drawer fronts.

5 ~ Glue on knobs of shaped modelling material.

Modesty Screen

You will need ~
Trace of 1 template
Wood strip
Wood stain
4 rub-down transfers
Masking tape

1 ~ Transfer trace of template to wood strip and cut out 4 panels. If desired, stain.

2 ~ When dry, apply transfer to each panel. Use masking tape to hold panels together.

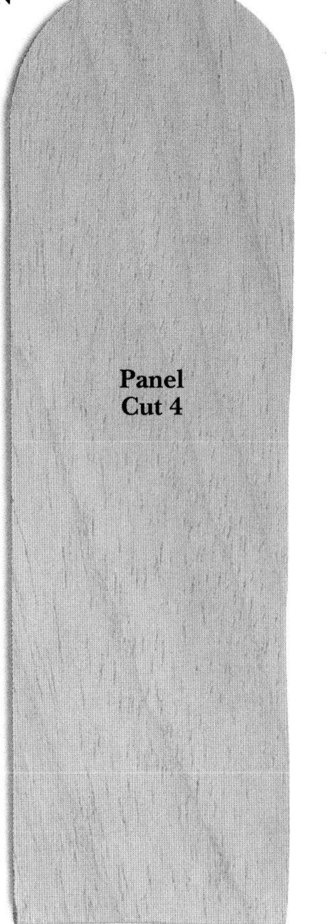

Small Rectangular Table

You will need ~
Traces of 4 templates
Squared strip
Wood strip
Tea for stain, optional
Glue
Modelling medium or bead for knob

1 ~ Transfer traced templates to wood strip and cut 1 top, 4 sides and a drawer front. Cut 4 pieces of squared strip to length shown for legs. Stain pieces with tea before glueing, if desired.

2 ~ Glue the two long and two short sides together to form a rectangular support for the top. Glue the top to the support.

3 ~ Carefully glue one leg into each corner.

4 ~ Add the drawer front and glue on a knob of modelling medium, painted, if necessary, or small bead.

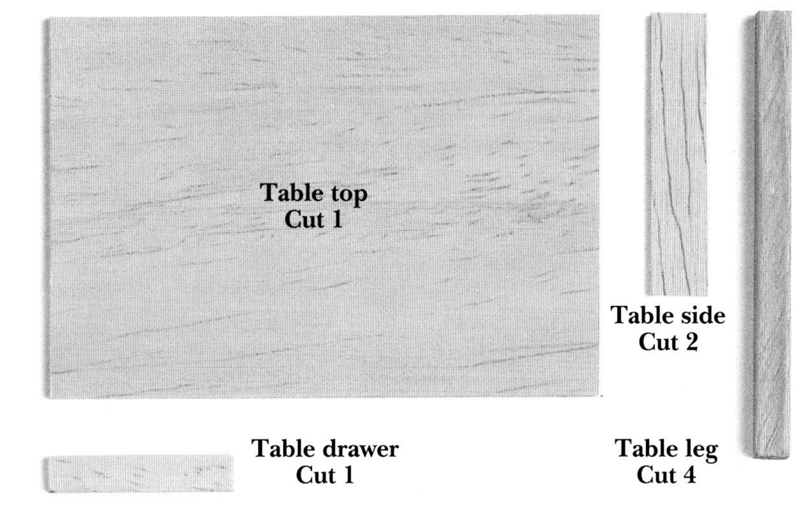

Plant Stand

You will need ~
Traces of 3 templates
Wood strip
Squared strip
Glue
Wood stain

1 ~ Transfer traces and cut top, shelf, and 4 sides from wood strip. Smooth ends with sandpaper wrapped around a pencil.

2 ~ Cut 4 legs from squared strip to length shown. Stain all pieces as desired.

3 ~ When the pieces are dry, glue the sides underneath the top then glue each leg into a corner. Add the shelf approximately two-thirds the way down the legs.

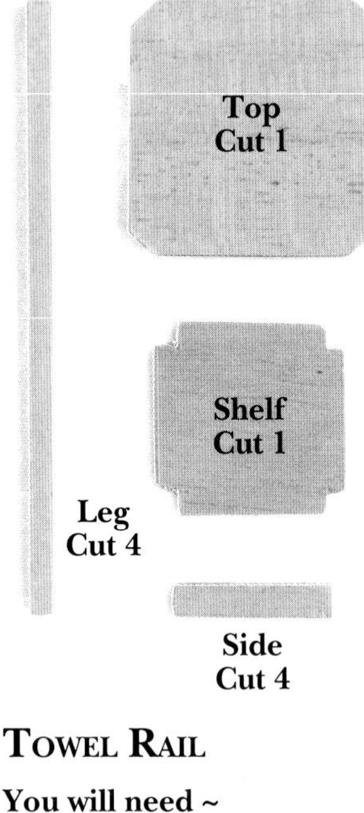

Chair back
Cut 2

Fold along lines

Towel Rail

You will need ~
Traces of 1 template
Wood strip
Wood stain
Dowel
Glue

1 ~ Transfer trace of side to wood strip and cut out.

2 ~ If edges are rough, take a piece of sandpaper, wrap it around a pencil, and use this to finely shape the curved edges.

3 ~ Cut 4 pieces of dowel to the length shown for rails; sand the edges neatly.

4 ~ Apply stain and when dry, glue dowels in place, one along the bottom, one on top, and two opposing just beneath.

Side
Cut 2

Rail
Cut 4

Wing-Back Chair

You will need ~
Traces of 3 templates
Cardboard
Wadding
Glue
Fabric
Masking tape
Elastic band
Modelling medium or beads

1 ~ Transfer traces to cardboard and cut out 2 chair backs, making one slightly smaller than the other, 2 seats and a front.

2 ~ Score the larger chair back along black lines and bend forward.

3 ~ Using the back template, cut a piece of wadding 2.5 cm (1 in) larger all around. Glue wadding to the back, trimming it at the top but wrapping excess over chair "arms".

4 ~ Again, using the back template, cut out your chosen upholstery fabric, adding 2.5 cm (1 in) all around and use this to cover the wadding.

5 ~ Score the smaller back piece along black lines and bend slightly forward. Cover it in fabric. Right side facing outward, glue this back to the first one, making sure any excess fabric is well tucked in between the two.

6 ~ Cover one seat with wadding and fabric, tucking ends under and glueing.

Chair seat
Cut 2

Chair front
Cut 1

7 ~ Cover the front piece with some wadding and fabric.

8 ~ Cover the other seat piece with fabric. Sandwich the front between both seats, the padded one on top, and glue together. Apply glue around sides and back of seat and slot into back. Hold all pieces together with an elastic band until the glue sets.

9 ~ Make legs of modelling medium or use wooden beads. Attach to base.

Settee

You will need ~
Traces of 3 templates
Cardboard
Tape
Wadding
Fabric
Elastic band
Card
Beads
Braid or other trim

1 ~ For the base, transfer the traced template to cardboard and cut out; score along the black lines. Fold the base into a box shape. Use tape to reinforce the corners. Cut a piece of wadding to fit the seat area and glue in place. Cover the base with your fabric, as neatly as possible, tucking the edges in well out of sight.

2 ~ To make the back, transfer the traced template to cardboard and cut out two. Use the same template to cut a piece of wadding to fit. Glue the wadding onto one back. Using the back template but adding 2.5 cm (1 in) all around, cut out 2 pieces of your fabric and use one to cover back. Tuck edges well in. Trim 2 mm (1/16 in) all around the perimeter of the second back piece and glue on other piece of fabric. Snip away any excess fabric and, keeping the padded side to the front, glue the other back to it, right sides facing outwards.

3 ~ For the arms, transfer the traced template to cardboard and cut out 2; score along black lines. Glue on some wadding. Fold your fabric in half right sides facing and, using the arm template, cut out two coverings, adding 12 mm (1/2 in) all around. Stitch the fabric on two sides to form a sleeve. Turn right side out and insert the padded arm piece. Sew up the third side.

4 ~ To assemble the settee, fit the base to the back and the arms to the base and back. Take note where surfaces meet and, when you are happy with the shape and fit, apply a thin line of glue along these meeting places. Press the pieces together firmly, and use your elastic band to hold them in place until the glue has set.

5 ~ To neaten the base, cut a piece of card to the shape and cover it with fabric. Glue it to the bottom of the base. Attach the beads to form a foot on each corner. Apply braid or other trim around edges.

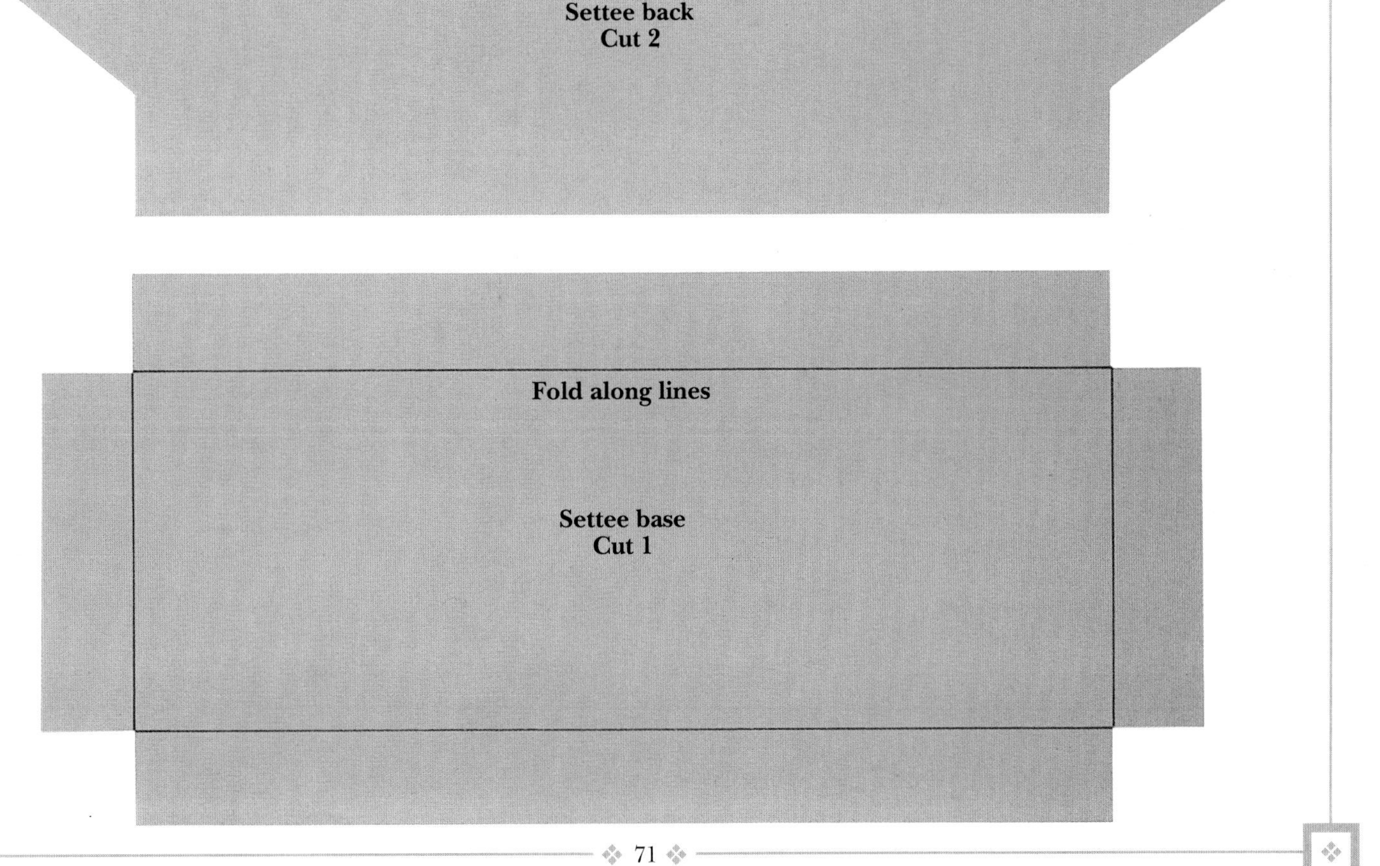

Round Table

You will need ~
Traces of 2 templates
Cardboard
Tape
Glue
Fabric

1 ~ Transfer traces to cardboard, making two base pieces, and cut out.

2 ~ Starting at the top of each base, cut out a notch in the centre, approximately 2 mm ($^{1}/_{16}$ in) wide and 30 mm ($1^{1}/_{8}$ in) long, stopping about 25 mm (1 in) from the end.

3 ~ Slot one base into the other forming an intersecting support. If necessary, use tape to strengthen join.

4 ~ Glue circular table top to base. When firmly set, cut out a piece of fabric, 17.5 cm (7 in) in diameter, and attach to the table top. If you like, cover this with a smaller circular lacy piece, approximately 11 cm ($4^{1}/_{4}$ in) in diameter.

Table top
Cut 1

Table base
Cut 2

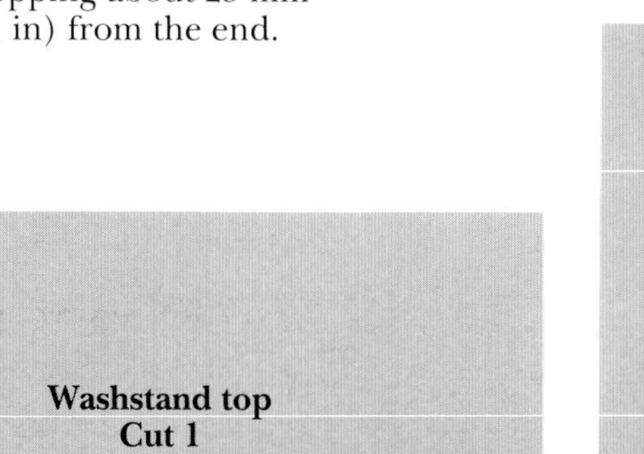

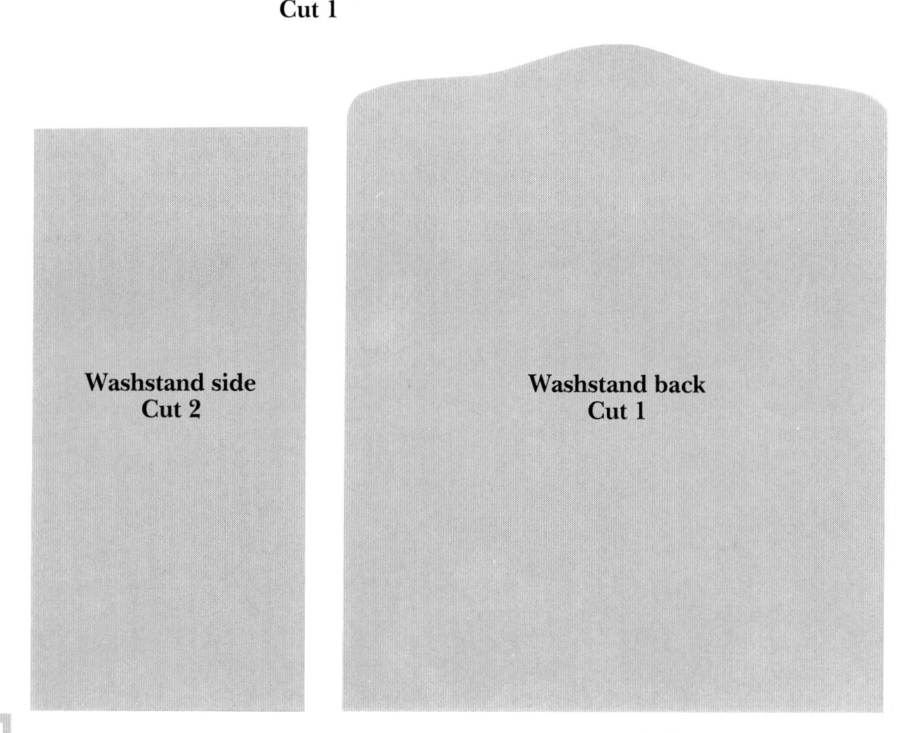

Washstand top
Cut 1

Washstand shelf
Cut 1

Overhang
Cut 1

Washstand side
Cut 2

Washstand back
Cut 1

Washstand

You will need ~
Traces of 5 templates
Cardboard
Glue
Acrylic primer and paint

1 ~ Transfer traces to cardboard and cut out 2 sides, back, top, shelf and overhang.

2 ~ Glue sides to back; add top, overhang, and shelf.

3 ~ Cover with primer and then, when dry, paint.

4 ~ Apply paint in blobs to get raised decorative effect for the ends of the overhang and in the middle of the curved back.

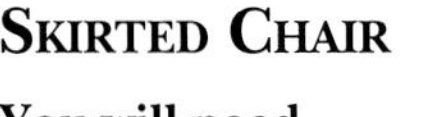

Skirted Chair

You will need ~
Traces of 4 templates
Cardboard
Wadding
Glue
Fabric and ribbon trim
Tape

1 ~ Transfer traced templates to cardboard and cut out. Using front template, cut out wadding and glue to front. Cover with fabric.

2 ~ Cover the back with fabric and, wrong sides facing, glue the back to the front, making certain any excess fabric is covered.

3 ~ Cut a circle of fabric, 15 cm (6 in) in diameter. If you like, paint the edge with fabric sealer to keep it from fraying.

4 ~ Take the base piece and tape the ends so it makes a 45 mm ($1^3/_4$ in) diameter cylinder.

5 ~ To the chair seat, glue a piece of wadding cut to the same size. Fix seat to top of base and glue fabric piece over it so that it drapes.

6 ~ Add ribbon trim along the edge of the seat; glue base piece to chair back.

Doll's House

You will need ~
Traces of 4 templates
Single-ply plywood
Acrylic primer and paint
Glue
Fabric
Beads
Tape

1 ~ Transfer traces of templates to plywood and cut out 2 backs, 2 sides, the roof and 2 floors, and the base. On one back cut out windows and door to make a front.

2 ~ Paint the exterior and interior and glue fabric scraps to "walls", "floors", and "attic ceiling". Attach the sides of the house to the back, and the base to the sides.

3 ~ Glue in the floors and attach the roof pieces.

4 ~ Add any tiny pieces of furniture of painted wood, beads, fabric, or modelling medium to the interior.

5 ~ Paint the front of the house appropriately, picking out window boxes and trailing roses, and when dry, decorate the reverse side, paying particular attention to window treatments.

6 ~ Attach the front with transparent tape "hinges".

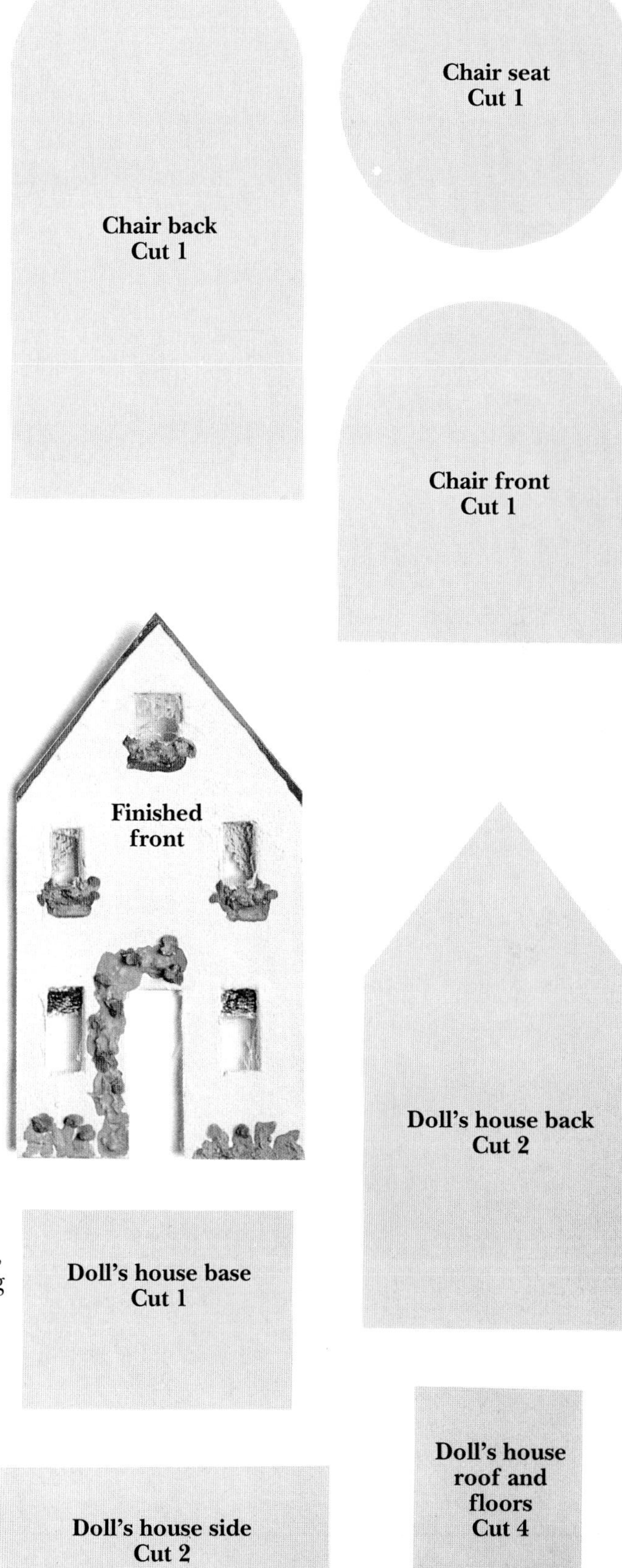

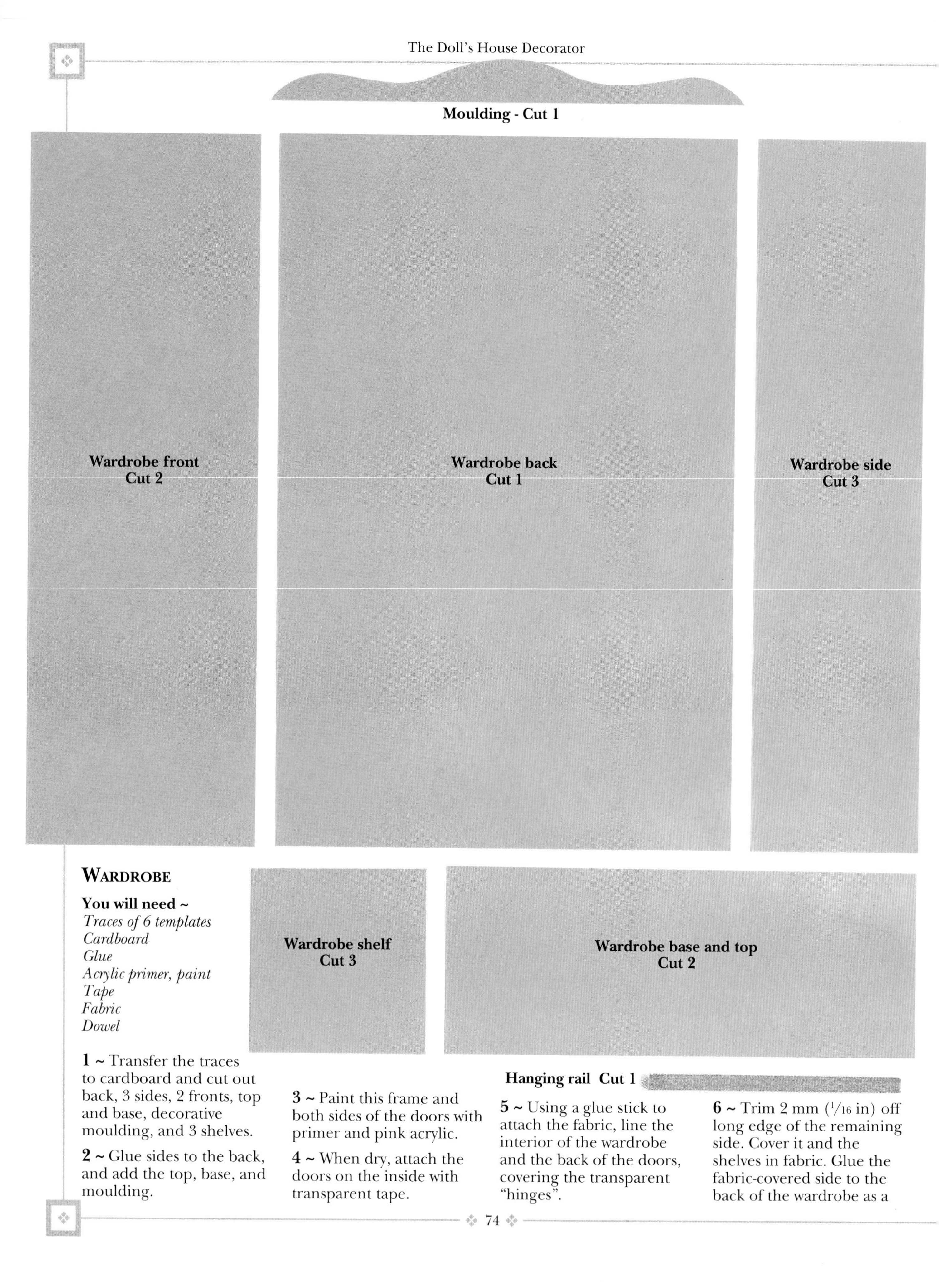

Wardrobe

You will need ~
Traces of 6 templates
Cardboard
Glue
Acrylic primer, paint
Tape
Fabric
Dowel

1 ~ Transfer the traces to cardboard and cut out back, 3 sides, 2 fronts, top and base, decorative moulding, and 3 shelves.

2 ~ Glue sides to the back, and add the top, base, and moulding.

3 ~ Paint this frame and both sides of the doors with primer and pink acrylic.

4 ~ When dry, attach the doors on the inside with transparent tape.

5 ~ Using a glue stick to attach the fabric, line the interior of the wardrobe and the back of the doors, covering the transparent "hinges".

6 ~ Trim 2 mm (1/16 in) off long edge of the remaining side. Cover it and the shelves in fabric. Glue the fabric-covered side to the back of the wardrobe as a

Chest of Drawers

You will need ~
Traces of 4 templates
Wood strip
Wood stain
8 pearls

1 ~ Transfer traced templates to wood and cut out front, back, 2 sides, top, and 4 drawers.

2 ~ With sandpaper wrapped round a pencil, smooth bottom edge of front; stain pieces as desired.

3 ~ Glue the sides to the back and the front to the sides. Add the top.

4 ~ Starting 4mm (1/8 in) from top, glue on "drawers" 4mm (1/8 in) apart. Add pearls for knobs.

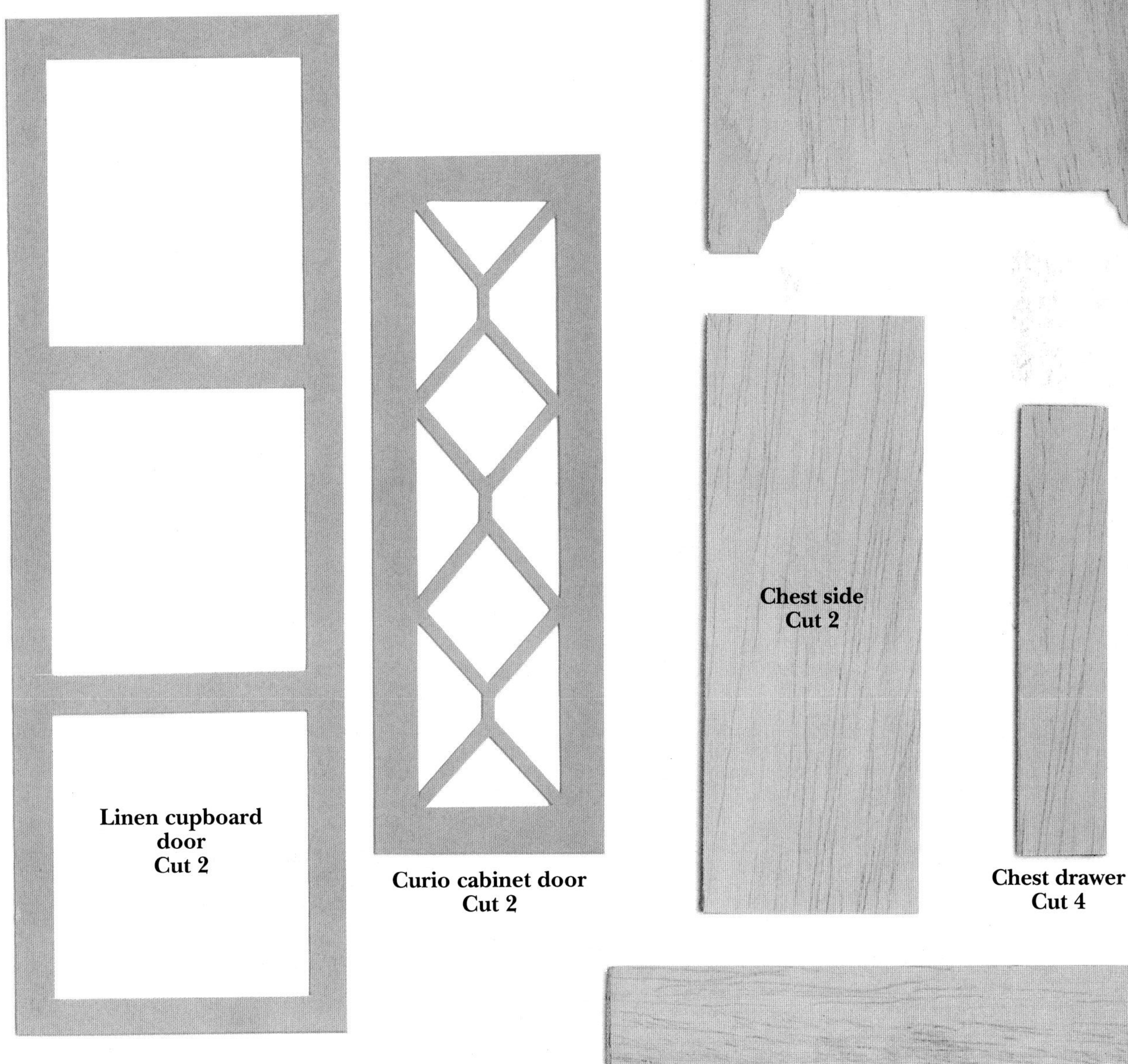

support for the shelves. Glue in the three shelves.

7 ~ Cut dowel to length shown and glue in 12 mm (1/2 in) down from top on left side as hanging rail.

8 ~ Paint on further decoration to the front of the wardrobe doors and top moulding. A blob of paint should serve as the door knobs.

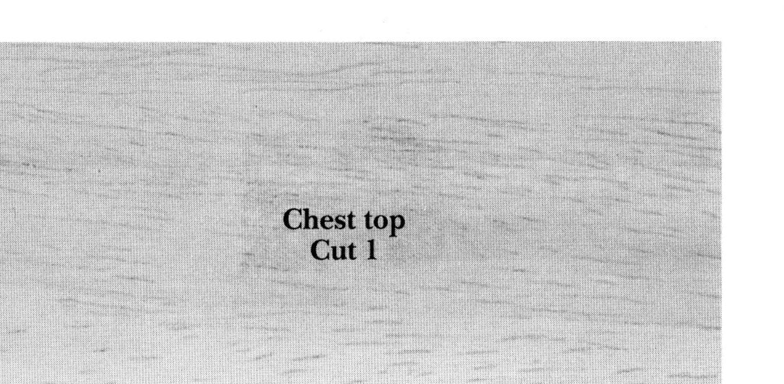

Bed base
Cut 1

Fold along lines

Headboard
(Inner rectangle)
Cut 2

4-Poster Bed

You will need ~

Traces of 3 templates
Cardboard
Fabric
Tape
Glue
Lace and ribbon trim
Dowel
Paint

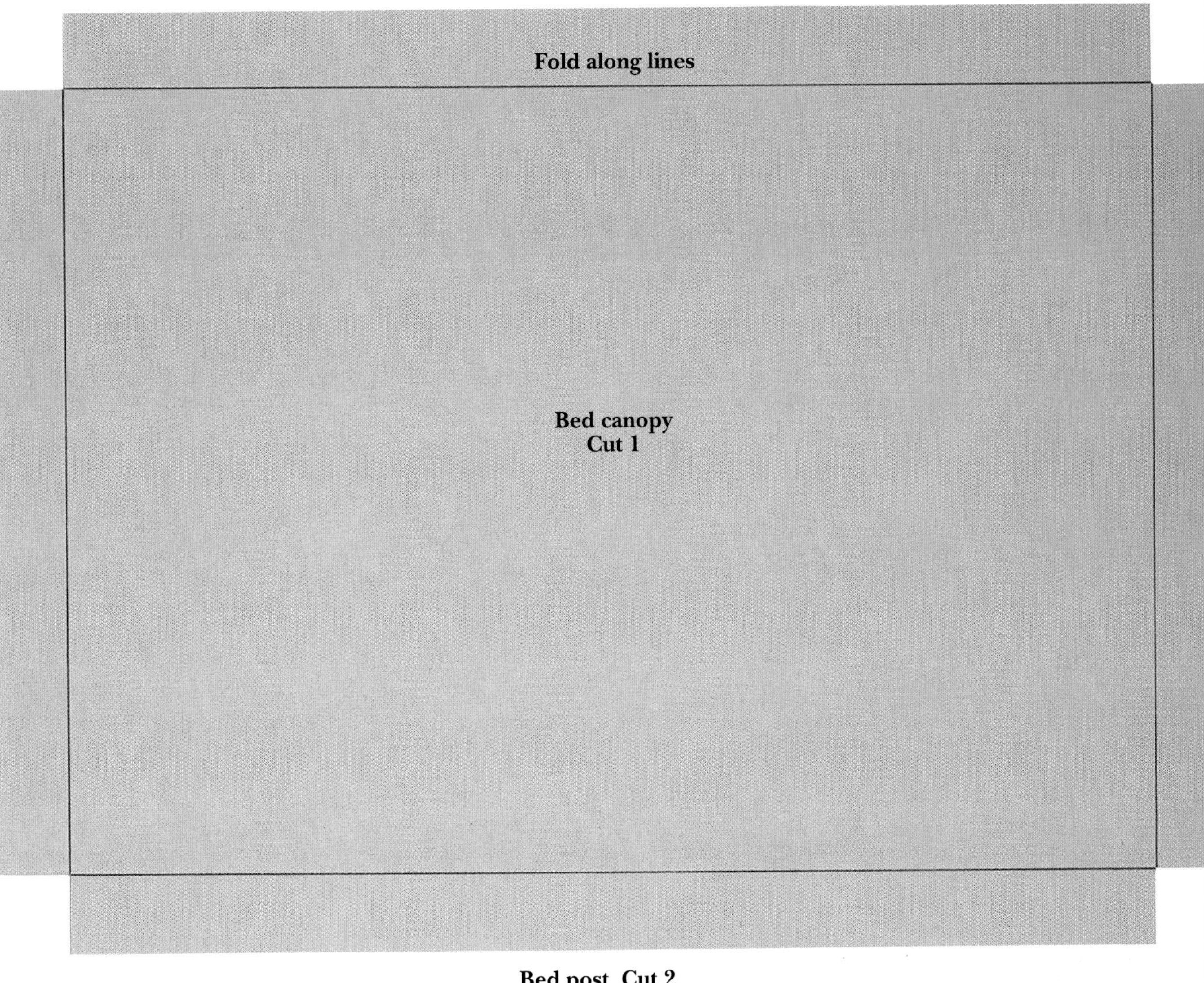

Create the Base

1 ~ Transfer larger trace to cardboard. Score along black lines and fold down, holding the corners together with tape.

2 ~ For the "valance": hem one end of a 100 x 10 cm (40 x 4 in) piece of fabric and then gather it at the other end so a ruffled edge is formed. Glue valance to the centre of the base.

3 ~ To hold the valance in place, cut another piece of cardboard, the same size as the top of the base, cover with a matching piece of fabric, and glue it firmly in place over the top.

Make the Headboard

1 ~ Transfer trace to 2 pieces of cardboard. Cover both with fabric.

2 ~ Attach one fabric-covered piece to the top end of the bed's base. Set the other headboard piece aside for later.

Form the Canopy

1 ~ Transfer trace to cardboard. Score along black lines and fold down, holding the corners together with tape.

2 ~ Cover with fabric, tucking the edges in at the corners and glue fabric to underside of canopy.

3 ~ For the frill: hem one end of a 100 x 5 cm (40 x 2 in) piece of fabric and then gather it at the other end so a ruffled edge is formed. Glue this to the inside edge of the canopy so it faces right side out.

4 ~ To neaten the canopy and help hold the frill in place, cut another piece of cardboard, the same size as the top of the canopy, cover with a matching piece of fabric, and glue it firmly in place to the underside.

5 ~ Add a strip of lace all around the underside of the frill. Glue a strip of embroidered flower trim all around the perimeter of the canopy.

Add the Drapes

1 ~ Cut two pieces of fabric 5 x 19 cm (2 x 7½ in); make a 6 mm (¼ in) hem on all sides and glue lace trim to one long end of each piece.

2 ~ Take the untrimmed long end of each "drape" and glue it to the back of the headboard, about 6mm (¼ in) in.

3 ~ Then attach the second fabric-covered headboard piece, right side out, so the drapes are

The Bed Clothes

Coverlet has quilted diamonds and pearls set into the points

"Woollen" blanket is felt with embroidered detail

Sheets are fine cotton or linen handkerchiefs

Mattress is wadding covered in cotton material

carefully and neatly sandwiched between the two headboard pieces.

Assemble the bed

1 ~ Cut 2 bed posts from dowel to length shown. If you like, paint the dowel or cover with fabric or ribbon.

2 ~ Insert the end of each dowel into the bed base (making a slight hole in the fabric) 6 mm (1/4 in) in from the end of the bed.

3 ~ Set the canopy on top of the dowels and headboard. Glue, if necessary.

Kitchen Stove

You will need ~
Traces of 11 templates
Cardboard
Masking tape
Glue
Acrylic primer and black paint
Split peas
Gold paint
Tile-decorated paper
Gold stars
Tissue paper: red, orange, yellow and black

1 ~ Transfer all the template shapes to cardboard. Cut out shapes.

2 ~ Using masking tape, join the major pieces of the stove – the two outer sides to the back, the front to the sides, and the inner sides (at the edge of the "grate" on the front) to the back.

3 ~ Slot in the shelf and top of the stove. Assemble the ash box.

4 ~ When you are happy with the fit, glue the pieces together.

5 ~ Glue on the "oven doors" and "drawers".

6 ~ Paint the entire unit with the black acrylic paint; paint the split peas with gold paint.

7 ~ When the stove is dry, attach the tile-decorated paper to the splashback – the back and sides of the stove – and the gold split-pea "knobs" to the drawers and doors.

8 ~ Cut 4 "hinges" from gold stars and attach 2 to the outer side of each oven door.

9 ~ Fill the ash box with crumpled tissue paper and tape it to the inner sides so it is held securely.

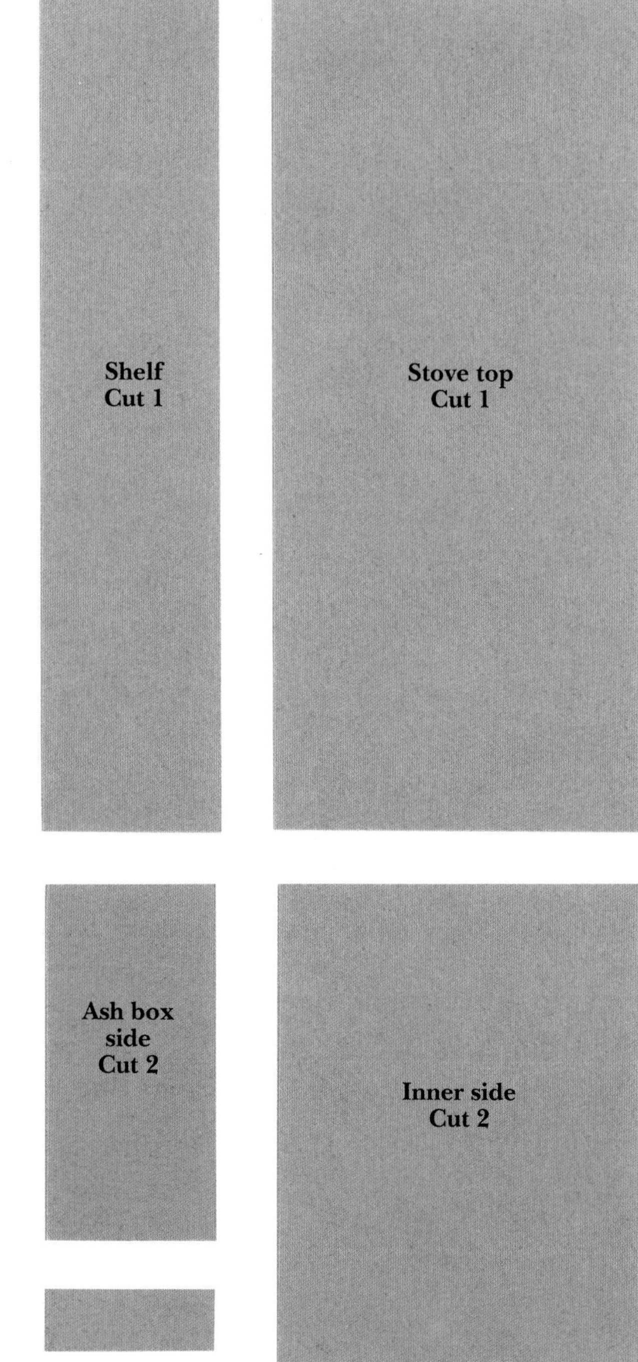

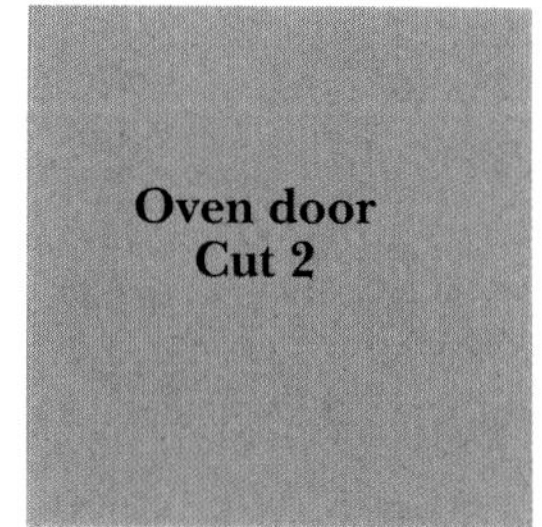

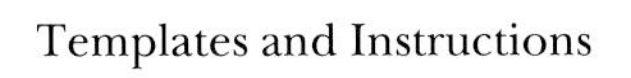

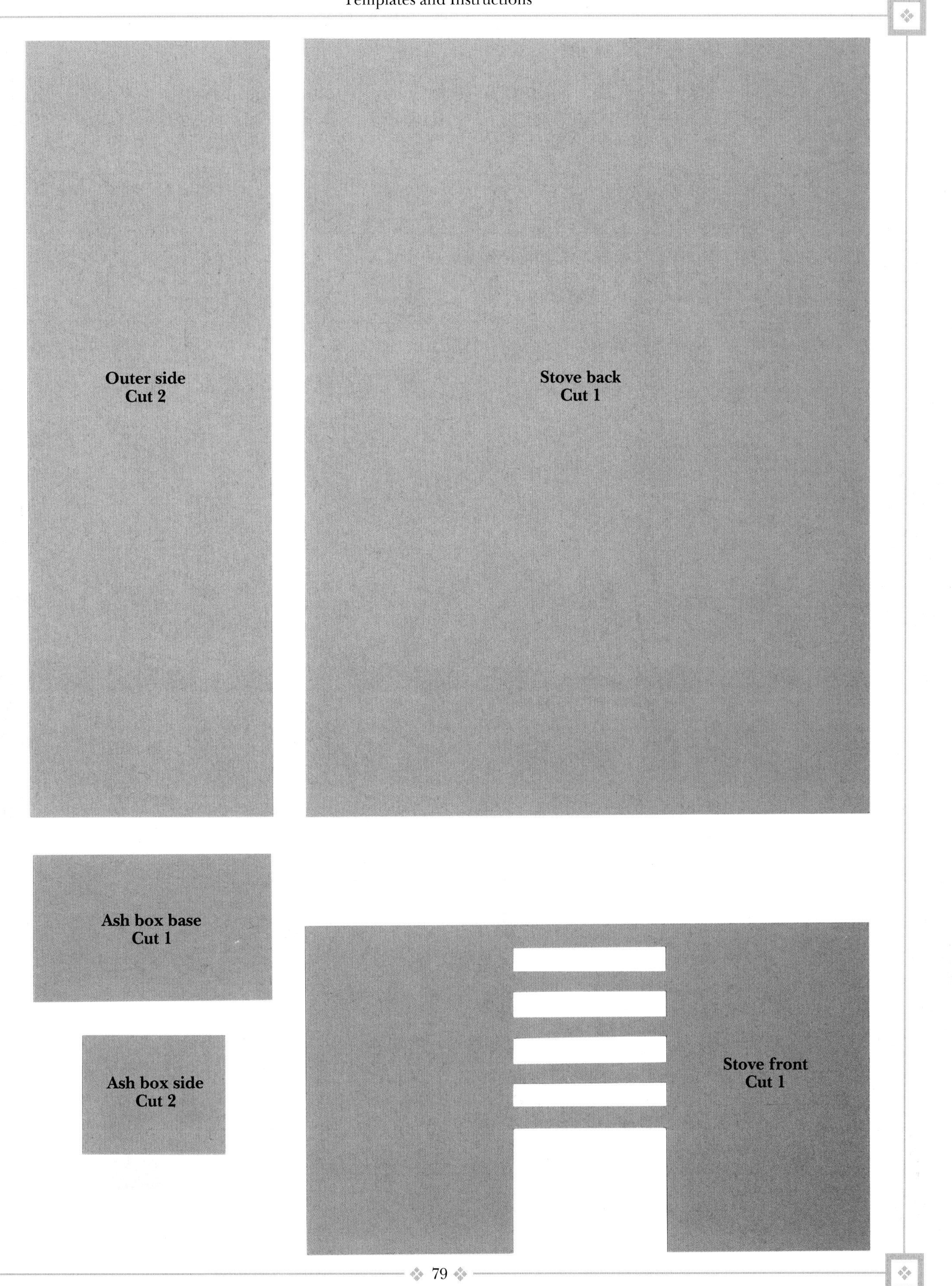
Outer side
Cut 2
Stove back
Cut 1
Ash box base
Cut 1
Ash box side
Cut 2
Stove front
Cut 1

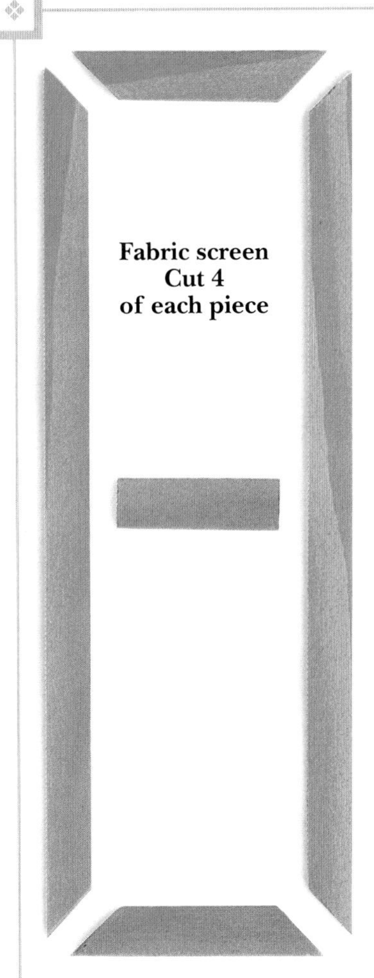
Fabric screen
Cut 4
of each piece

Corner Shelf

You will need ~
Traces of 5 templates
Wood strip
Sandpaper
Wood stain
Glue

1 ~ Transfer traces to wood strip and cut out 2 sides and 4 shelves.

2 ~ Using sandpaper wrapped around a pencil, smooth the curves. Stain pieces as desired.

3 ~ Glue one side along the edge of the other side. Glue in shelves approximately 2.5 cm (1 in) apart.

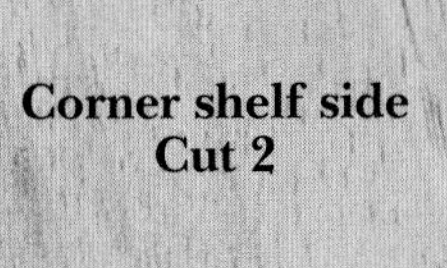
Corner shelf side
Cut 2

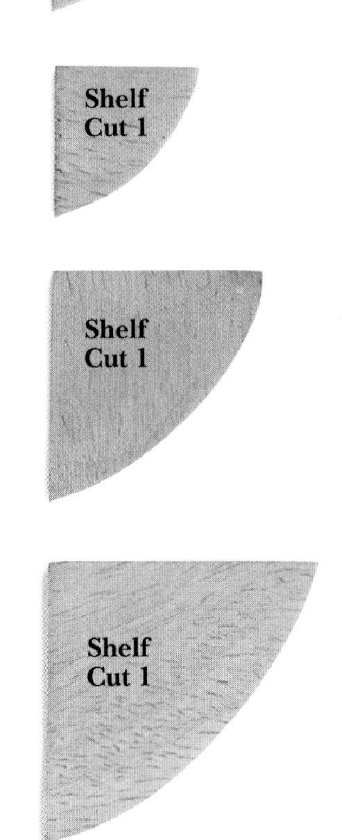
Shelf
Cut 1

Shelf
Cut 1

Shelf
Cut 1

Shelf
Cut 1

Fabric Screen

You will need ~
Traces of 5 templates
Wood strip
Glue and wallpaper glue
Fabric
Transparent tape

1 ~ Transfer traces to wood and cut out four panels. Join the pieces to form a rectangle with central strip.

2 ~ Cut 4 pieces of fabric the length of each frame but twice the width.

3 ~ Paint fabric with wallpaper glue and pleat to fit the frame. Let dry and glue to back of each frame.

4 ~ Tape along the back to join frames together.

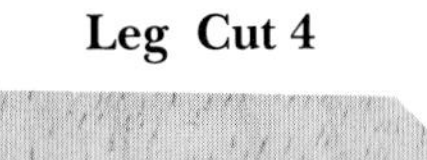
Leg Cut 4

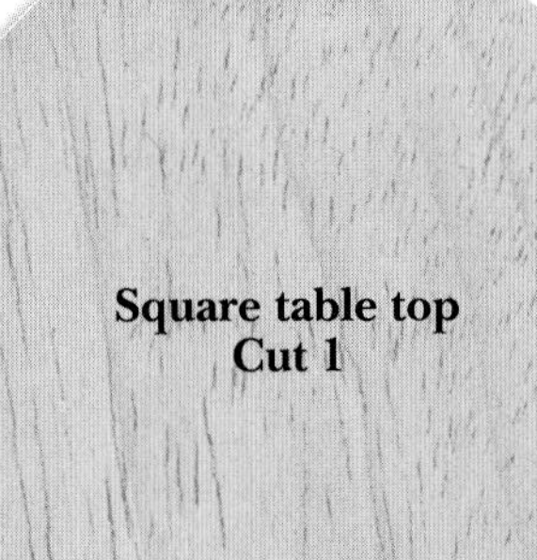
Square table top
Cut 1

Side piece Cut 4

Cross piece
Cut 4

Small Square Table

You will need ~
Traces of 2 templates
Wood strip
Squared strip
Glue
Wood stain

1 ~ Transfer traced templates and cut out top and 4 sides from wood strip. Cut 4 legs and 4 cross pieces from squared strip to the lengths shown.

2 ~ Stain pieces as desired.

3 ~ Glue sides to underneath of top.

4 ~ Glue a leg in each corner; glue cross pieces between the legs.

Wooden Chair

You will need ~
Traces of 3 templates
Wood strip
Squared strip
Wood stain
Glue

1 ~ Transfer traces to wood strip and cut out seat, 6 sides, and 4 cross pieces. Cut 4 legs from squared strip to the lengths shown.

2 ~ Stain pieces as desired.

3 ~ Position seat about halfway down and glue to the back legs and the tops of the front legs.

4 ~ Glue 4 side pieces in between legs under seat. Glue 2 side pieces as slats between back legs. Glue cross pieces near bottom of legs.

Chair seat
Cut 1

Back leg
Cut 2

Side piece
Cut 6

Front leg
Cut 2

Cross piece
Cut 4